DATE DUE

DE 18 '99			
FE 16 '00			
De 15 '00			
JE 28 '01			
AG 9 '01			
JE 11 '02			
AG 8 '02			
JA 30 '03			
FE 13 '03			
JE 9 '04			
AC 3 '05			
AG 13 '09 AG 3 1 '09			

DEMCO 38-296

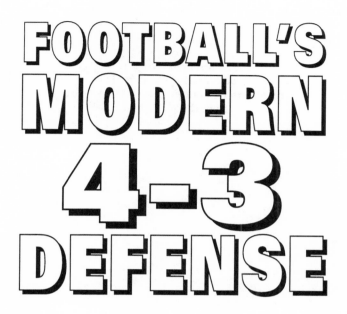

FOOTBALL'S MODERN 4-3 DEFENSE

Bob Kenig

Harding Press
Haworth, New Jersey 07641

Library of Congress Cataloging-in-Publication Data
Kenig, Bob, 1946–
    Football's modern 4-3 defense / Bob Kenig.
        p.   cm.
    ISBN 0-9624779-9-0
    1. Football—Defense.   I. Title.
    GV951.18.K48   1997
    796.332'2—dc21   96-52881
                                                          CIP

ISBN: 0-9624779-9-0

Printed in the United States of America

HARDING PRESS
P. O. Box 141
Haworth, NJ 07641
Books by and for the coaching profession

This book is dedicated to Lou Bonder.

Mr. Bonder was: My High School Football Coach.

The Athletic Director who hired me for my first football coaching position.

My mentor.

The person who instilled in me the burning desire to be a football coach.

The person who made me play far above my ability.

Along with my father, the person who I always went to with a problem.

The most prepared person I ever knew.

The person whose office I went to everyday, just to talk.

In every sense of the word, a WINNER!

I truly miss him. I often go to his grave to have our talks, and I am sure he still listens and guides me.

In Heaven, where God is the Athletic Director, I know Lou Bonder is the High School Football Coach. I know this because God would only select the BEST.

Contents

PART II
FRONT AND SECONDARY VARIATIONS   47

PART III
THE 4-3 DEFENSE IN ACTION   109

Part I

The Basic 4-3 Defense

1

Getting Ready to Employ the 4-3 Defense

The 4-3 Defense, in some form, was predominantly the defense of choice in the NFL for many years. This was somewhat altered in the seventies and eighties with the introduction and use of the 3-4 Defense, which is a variation of the Oklahoma 5-2 Defense. With the tremendous success of the Jimmy Johnson- and Barry Switzer-coached Dallas Cowboys and their use of the 4-3 Defense, it seems most of the NFL teams have returned to the 4-3.

The success of the University of Miami, under Johnson, encouraged many colleges that were not already using the 4-3 Defense to give it a try. Today, the 4-3 is used by so many college teams, it is jokingly referred to as "The NCAA Defense."

The defensive package presented in this book is primarily the 4-3 Defense employed at Widener University. The Widener defensive scheme is based upon the 4-3 defenses of the University of Miami and the Dallas Cowboys. There are several facets of the Widener University 4-3 Defense that were developed specifically for the type of defensive personnel playing at Widener and for the opponents Widener faces. These wrinkles may not be used by all proponents of the 4-3 Defense, but they have proven to be very successful at Widener University and are consistent with the basic concepts of the 4-3 Defense.

This chapter establishes a foundation upon which a total understanding of all aspects of the 4-3 Defense can be built.

DEFINING DEFENSIVE AREAS

Gaps and Areas on the Field

Each member of the defensive front seven is responsible for a gap versus the running game and the blitzing game. The four down linemen are responsible to rush certain gaps versus the pass. In order for the defenders to easily identify these offensive gaps, they are named as follows:

1. Between the center and guards—"A" Gap
2. Between the guards and tackles—"B" Gap
3. Between the tackles and tight end (or tight slot) and outside the tackle to a split-end side—"C" Gap
4. Outside the tight end (or tight slot)—"D" Gap (Diagram 1-1)

DIAGRAM 1–1

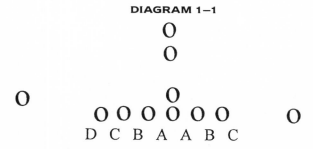

As in all defensive schemes, the front seven in the 4-3 Defense align on landmarks established on the offensive players. For example, rather than telling a defensive tackle to align on the outside shoulder of the guard, the guard position is broken down to three different landmarks, and the defensive tackle is told to align on one of these landmarks. For simplicity, these landmarks are numbered. The following are those landmarks:

1. Head on the center—0
2. On either shoulder of the center—1
3. Head on the guard—2
4. On the inside shoulder of the guard—2i
5. On the outside shoulder of the guard—3
6. Head on the tackle—4

7. On the inside shoulder of the tackle—4i
8. On the outside shoulder of the tackle—5
9. Head on the tight end (or tight slot)—6
10. On the inside shoulder of the tight end (or tight slot)—6i
11. On the outside shoulder of the tight end (or tight slot)—7
12. Outside the tight end (or tight slot)—9 (Diagram 1-2)

DIAGRAM 1–2

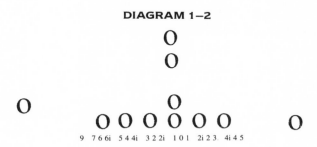

For the purpose of pass-coverage responsibilities, the field is divided into various zones, and these are given specific names. These zones use the line of scrimmage and the ball as the starting points. Although specific measurements are attached to these areas, from game to game these measurements may slightly vary. The zones also vary according to the pass coverage being employed. For example, when a two-deep zone coverage is used, there are two deep and five short zones named. However, when a three-deep zone coverage is employed, there are three deep and four short zones. In Chapter 7, this is covered in much greater detail.

Positions

For a basic understanding of the 4-3 Defense, this section presents a brief description of the defensive positions. However, for a total understanding of the 4-3 Defense, more detailed descriptions occur in Chapters 3, 4, and 5.

- *Tackle:* A down lineman who normally aligns in a 1, 2i, or 3 alignment.
- *End:* A down lineman who normally aligns in a 5, 6i, 7, or 9 alignment.

Note: When the number "0" follows the numbered landmark, it indicates the linebacker positions. The linebackers use the same landmarks as the down lineman but usually align from three to five yards off the line of scrimmage.

- *Middle linebacker:* A two-point stance defender who normally aligns in a 20i to 20i alignment. This is determined by the offensive formation.
- *Outside linebacker–Strongside (Sam):* A two-point stance defender who normally aligns in a 50, 60i, or 7 alignment.
- *Outside linebacker–Weakside (Will):* A two-point stance defender who normally aligns in a 50, 60i, or 7 alignment.
- *Safety–Strongside (Strong):* A two-point stance defender who normally aligns off the ball to the strongside of the offensive formation.
- *Safety–Weakside (Free):* A two-point stance defender who normally aligns off the ball to the weakside of the offensive formation.
- *Corners:* Two-point stance defenders who normally align off the ball and are the widest defenders in the secondary. (Diagram 1-3)

DIAGRAM 1–3

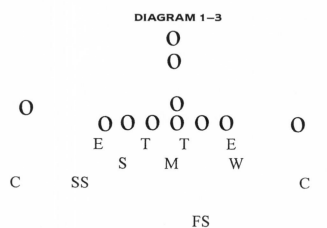

Formation Strength

The 4-3 Defense uses the strength of the offensive formation to determine alignments. For this reason, it is crucial to establish rules to determine formation strength. The following are the basic strength rules; these may change due to particular game plans.

DIAGRAM 1—4

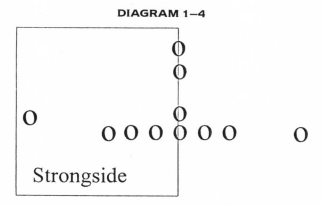

For the secondary, the strongside of the formation is the one with the most possible receivers. Versus a Pro formation, the strongside is the flanker/tight-end side. (Diagram 1-4) In a Trips formation, the strong-side is the three-receiver side of the formation. (Diagram 1-5)

DIAGRAM 1—5

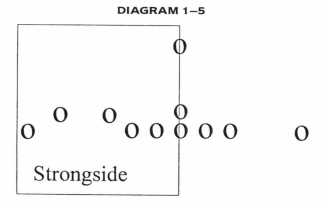

When an offense has a truly balanced formation, like a Double-Slot formation, the strength is determined by the position on the field. When the ball is on the hash mark, strength is declared to the wide side of the field. (Diagram 1-6) When the ball is in the middle of the field, strength is declared to the defensive left.

For the defensive front, strength is determined by the alignment of the tight end. The tight-end side is always the strongside. (Diagram 1-7) However, when there is no tight end, the strength rules for the secondary apply to the front.

DIAGRAM 1—6

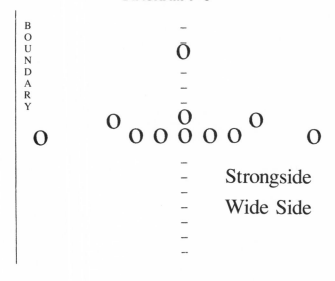

DIAGRAM 1—7

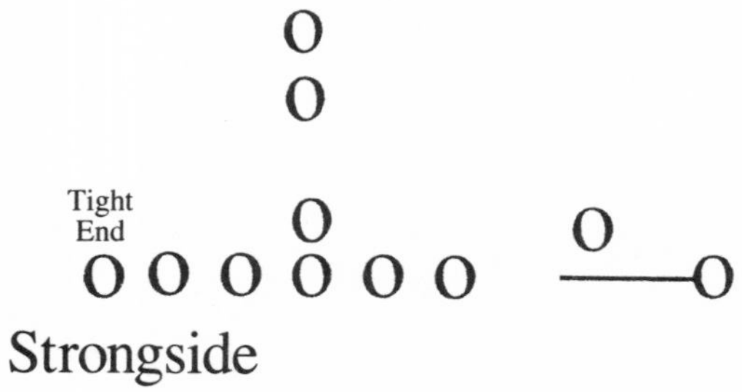

CALLING THE DEFENSE

The defense is called in the following manner:

1. The Front
2. The Stunt, if one is being employed
3. The Blitz, if one is being employed
4. The Coverage

Examples of calls are as follows:

- *40–Silver:* The front is in a basic 40 alignment and the secondary is employing a Silver coverage.

- *40 Weak–Stem–Orange:* The front is going to initially align in 40. The stunt is Stem. Stem tells the front they are going to move to a 40 Weak prior to the snap of the ball. The secondary is employing an Orange coverage.

- *40 Flop–7 Blitz–Red:* The front aligns in a 40 Flop alignment and executes a 7 Blitz on the snap of the ball. The secondary is employing a Red coverage.

DISGUISE

Using various methods of disguising the defense is certainly not unique to the 4-3 Defense. With the changes in offensive football, disguises have become a necessity for the successful defensive coach. Offenses have become much more sophisticated, with well-coached quarterbacks who have been taught to make pre-snap reads and to either adjust the called play from this read or to audible to a new play. The Modern 4-3 Defense has these disguises built into the defensive scheme.

A method of disguise employed at Widener University is the "Show and Trick" disguise. When a Blitz is employed, the Blitz may be called with or without the word "Show" following the Blitz call. When the Blitz is called without "Show," it is executed with the linebackers blitzing from their normal alignment. The secondary is in some type of man-to-man coverage with the defenders aligned to look as though a zone coverage is being used.

When "Show" follows the Blitz call, the linebackers align on the line of scrimmage in the gaps they intend to blitz. The secondary aligns in a man-to-man coverage and the corners align on the receivers they are covering.

When "Trick" follows the front call, the linebackers align in the same alignment as "Show." They align on the line of scrimmage giving an indication of Blitz. The secondary also aligns as though "Show" is called. On the snap of the ball, or immediately prior to the anticipated snap, the defenders move to the normal alignment dictated by the defensive call.

By using the Show and Trick disguise, the defense prohibits the quarterback from making an accurate pre-snap read. The quarterback cannot determine when a Blitz is coming. With so many offenses employing a set with a single running back and three wide receivers, the possibility of employing an audible against what is believed to be man-to-man coverage is totally eliminated.

This type of disguise was used by the University of Nebraska versus the University of Florida in the 1996 Fiesta Bowl, the National Championship Game. It was extremely effective in keeping the Gator offense off balance the entire game and helped lead Nebraska to the championship. The use of disguises is covered in more depth in Chapter 8.

2

Selecting Personnel for the 4-3 Defense

GENERAL PERSONNEL REQUIREMENTS

The type of personnel required to employ the 4-3 Defense suc-cessfully is similar to the personnel requirements for all modern defenses, with several specific exceptions.

Unlike many modern defensive schemes that look for size and strength first and speed second at the linebacker positions, the 4-3 requires speed first. This is especially true at the outside linebacker positions. The 4-3 interior personnel (tackles and ends) attempt to spill running plays to the outside, and the outside linebackers are expected to prevent the running back from turning the corner. From a size stand-point, the outside linebackers are often more like defensive backs than traditional outside linebackers.

Unlike a defensive scheme that employs an eight-man front with three defensive backs, the 4-3 Defense makes use of a seven-man front and four defensive backs. Any four-deep secondary scheme involves much more run support from members of the secondary than a three-deep scheme requires. This is particularly true of the 4-3. The safeties are, like the linebackers, expected to attack the wide running plays from the inside out and prevent the running back from turning the corner. These safeties are also expected to come up and attack any inside running play that breaks through the interior. Along with the ability to stop the run, the safeties are required to be excellent pass defenders and are expected to play both zone and man-to-man coverages. This applies to both the strong and free safety.

SITUATIONAL SUBSTITUTION

Because offensive football is making use of special personnel in particular situations, the 4-3 Defense is forced to use particular personnel to counteract any offensive advantage gained through substitution. Although true in many down-and-distance situations, it is particularly true in passing situations when the offense substitutes speedy wide receivers for the tight ends and running backs. The 4-3 defensive coach may substitute defensive backs for linebackers or defensive linemen to help cover these additional receivers. He may also replace the normal defensive ends with pass-rushing specialists. Any type of situational substitution allows the defensive coach the luxury of using specialists, whose talents are geared to certain situations and who are coached to handle these particular situations. It also allows more of the defensive personnel to become involved in the game.

Another personnel decision affecting the defensive coach is whether or not to play particular players to the strongside or weakside of the offensive formation. For example, should the defensive team have a strongside end and a weakside end or a left end and a right end? With so many offensive teams employing the tactic of changing strength prior to the snap of the ball, it is much more advisable to play with a left and a right player. This eliminates the problem of having players run to different positions prior to the snap. This can become quite a problem, especially for the down linemen. Having a right and left player at each position (except at middle linebacker, of course), allows both players to learn to play against the weakside and strongside of an offensive formation. Another advantage of this strategy is that only one competent player is required as a substitute for either position.

PARTICULAR POSITION REQUIREMENTS

The following description of the various 4-3 defensive positions contains those characteristics we would like each player to possess. However, we do not always find these characteristics. There is always that one player who is too small or too slow who, somehow, does an outstanding job. The particular position requirements are goals we would certainly like to attain for each position but may not always reach.

The following descriptions are for those positions used on regular down-and-distance situations. They do not include those specialists we employ in particular situations.

Tackles

The tackles are the two biggest and strongest members of the starting eleven. However, if the starting eleven defensive players are ranked in athletic ability, the tackles are normally the tenth- and eleventh-ranked players. It is hoped their size and strength can make up for their lack of athletic ability. The ideal situation is to have two defensive tackles who are larger and stronger than the guards and, therefore, create a mismatch. To have at least one tackle with size, strength, and good athletic ability is a real bonus. These two players are expected to be run stoppers and have the ability to collapse the pass pocket. Like all members of the defensive front, the defensive tackles must possess the discipline to read blocking schemes and react accordingly.

Ends

The ends are the fastest down defensive linemen and the best athletes. When looking for defensive tackles, size and strength are the most important characteristics. When looking for the correct personnel to play the defensive end position, speed and strength are more important than size. However, size cannot be overlooked and is still an important quality. The defensive ends should be better athletes and possess more quickness than the offensive tackles. These two offensive linemen are normally responsible for blocking the defensive ends, particularly in passing situations. Just as it is the desire of the defensive coach to have the defensive tackles mismatch the guards in size and strength, it is also his hope the defensive ends can mismatch the offensive tackles in athletic ability and speed. This mismatch can greatly aid in an effective pass rush and compensate for any lack of size versus the running game.

Middle Linebacker

The middle linebacker is the inside run stopper. Size, strength, and quickness are three requirements for this position. The ability to recognize formations and the intelligence to make defensive adjustment calls certainly cannot be overlooked. However, the most important requirement for this position is the ability to get to the ball on all running plays and to constantly make the big hits. The ability to cover the pass is also important, but not nearly as important as stopping the run. To have a middle linebacker who is equally effective against the run and the pass is the ideal situation. However, this is often not the case. In passing situations, the middle linebacker is normally the first player replaced due to situational substitution.

Outside Linebackers

Although size and strength cannot be ignored, the most important requirements for outside linebackers in the 4-3 Defense are speed and athleticism. These linebackers are not prototypical of most outside linebackers. They possess many more of the qualities of typical defensive backs than of typical linebackers.

Since it is the intent of the defensive scheme to spill all running plays to the outside, it is the job of the outside linebackers to prevent a running back from turning the corner. They are the players who are expected to have the ability to run down any running play while having the capability of being excellent pass defenders. The players who man these two positions could be the best two athletes in the defensive eleven.

Discipline is another requirement for this position. The outside linebacker, away from the initial movement of the ball in a running play, must hold his position to defend against the cutback or counter play. This is not a simple task for an aggressive athlete who desires to be in on every play.

Safeties

In the 4-3 Defense, there are two different safety positions, strong safety and free safety. It is a great advantage to have two similar athletes, each with the ability to play both positions. This eliminates the need to switch positions when an offense changes strength prior to the snap of the ball. However, this personnel luxury does not always occur. Therefore, the following is a description of the requirements for both positions.

The strong safety has many of the same requirements as the outside linebackers. The main difference between the two positions is speed. The strong safety needs to be faster and slightly more athletic than the outside linebackers. Like the outside linebackers, he is expected to be an excellent defender against the run. However, he is required to be a better pass defender than the outside linebackers. The ability to defend against the pass is often the quality that moves an outside linebacker candidate into the secondary.

The strong safety, in many secondary coverages, is the secondary defender employed to force the run. In some 4-3 defensive schemes, when a true strong safety cannot be found, two-deep coverage is often employed, and the corners, rather than the strong safety, become the secondary force defenders against the run. This allows the defense to play with two free safeties.

The free safety is often the best athlete in the defensive starting eleven. His ability to play pass defense is much more important than his ability to defend against the run. However, there are many situations when he is called upon to support the run, and this ability is certainly a requirement for this position. He needs more speed and range than the normal strong safety but does not require as much pure strength.

Intelligence is a requirement for all defensive personnel in the 4-3 Defense, but it is even more important for the free safety. He must possess the ability to recognize offensive formations and to make the proper calls to put the secondary and linebackers in the correct coverage. As the defender who makes so many crucial decisions and calls affecting the entire defensive unit, he has to be a player whose judgment and football knowledge are respected by his peers. He and the middle linebacker are normally the leaders of the defensive team.

Corners

The corners are the speedsters of the defensive unit. The main requirements for this position are speed and the ability to play both zone and man-to-man pass coverage. Unless a great deal of two-deep coverage is employed, the corners do not have to be great run stoppers. However, as with all the positions in the secondary, the ability to be an excellent open-field tackler is a prime requirement for this position.

In the past, the speedy little athlete could effectively play the corner position. Now, with so many offensive units employing bigger and more physical wide receivers, size has become a much more important requirement for the position of corner. The smaller, less physical corner is finding himself getting outmuscled or outjumped for the ball.

All secondary defenders must possess the ability to catch the football, and the corners are no exception to this rule. Turnovers have always been the key to winning football games. Without corners (and all defensive secondary members) who can effectively intercept the ball, the defensive coach is limiting the possibility of turnovers. This is especially true with so many offenses relying much more on the passing game than the running game. The days of taking the wide-receiver candidates with the poorest hands and putting them at the corner positions are long gone. These young men have to be as capable of catching passes as the wide receivers and much more physical.

3

The 4-3 Tackles and Ends

As briefly described in Chapter 1, the defensive front aligns according to landmarks established on the offensive players. When a down lineman is given the assignment of aligning on the shoulder of an offensive lineman, he is to align as close to the head of the offensive lineman as possible. The term "Nose On" is followed by the place on the offensive lineman where the defensive lineman is to align. When the strongside defensive tackle is told to use a 3 alignment, he is to align with his "Nose on the Outside Ear of the Guard." He may widen to the point where his "Nose Is on the Outside Shoulder of the Guard." The lineman must be in a position to defeat a straight-ahead block and protect his gap while not being susceptible to a reach block. For the 4-3 Defense to be effective, the defensive linemen can never get reached! The defensive lineman determines exactly where he has to align to accomplish both jobs. Normally, the quicker the defensive lineman, the closer he aligns to the head of the offensive lineman.

The defensive linemen normally employ a three-point stance. However, the defensive tackles may use a four-point stance if they are more effective with this stance. The defensive linemen align with the foot closest to the defender on whom they are aligned, slightly ahead of the other foot. The charge of a defensive lineman starts with this foot and it should be as close to the offensive lineman as possible. The defensive linemen align as close to the line of scrimmage as possible. In other words, they "crowd" the line of scrimmage.

TACKLES

Alignments

The strongside defensive tackle employs a 3 alignment on the strongside guard. (Diagram 3-1)

The weakside defensive tackle normally employs a 1 alignment to the weakside of the offensive formation. (Diagram 3-1) There are times, however, when he uses a 2i alignment on the weakside guard. The purpose for these alignment variations is covered in Part III of this book. (Diagram 3-1)

DIAGRAM 3—1

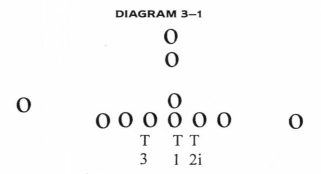

Techniques

The defensive tackle steps with the foot closest to the defender and aims this foot at an imaginary point directly below the head of the offensive lineman. He employs a "Straight-Arm Shiver" and attempts to get his hands under the breast plate of his opponent's shoulder pads. It is extremely important for the defender to keep his thumbs up and his fingers pointed out. This helps keep the elbows locked and maintains separation from the offensive blocker.

As the other foot is being moved forward, the tackle should be reading the block of the offensive player on whom he is aligned. He should react according to this block. It is extremely important to understand that the movement of the tackle is an attack. The tackle attacks the offensive lineman and reads on the run. The tackle does not sit and wait to see the blocking scheme. He must see it as he attacks it.

Reads and Reactions Vs.
Various Blocking Schemes

All defensive linemen read the helmet of the offensive lineman on whom they are aligned as their first key.

3 alignment

In this alignment, after the tackle reads the helmet of the guard, he feels for the offensive tackle's block and is aware of the path of the near back.

The main responsibility of the defensive tackle is to control the B gap versus a run in his direction. On a run away from him, the tackle squeezes the guard into the A gap. By forcing the guard into the A gap, the tackle protects the B gap and constricts the A gap. The tackle crosses the face of the guard only when the threat of cutback has disappeared, and he then pursues the play.

Versus a base block, the tackle takes his initial step and follows with the outside foot. He maintains proper leverage and controls the B gap. He squeezes the guard into the A gap and finds the football. (Diagram 3-2)

DIAGRAM 3—2

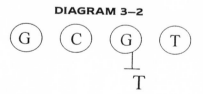

Versus the reach block, the tackle steps parallel to the line of scrimmage with his outside foot. He maintains outside leverage and widens while holding his position on the line of scrimmage. Remember, a defensive lineman in the 4-3 Defense can NEVER get reached. (Diagram 3-3)

DIAGRAM 3—3

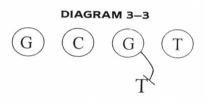

Versus a scoop block, the tackle anchors his outside foot and steps inside and parallel to the line of scrimmage with his inside foot, after his initial attack step. He attempts to keep the guard off the linebacker and avoids getting scooped by the tackle. (Diagram 3-4)

DIAGRAM 3—4

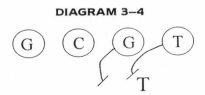

Versus the fold block, the tackle steps outside and parallel to the line of scrimmage with his outside foot. He squeezes the offensive tackle into the C gap and crosses his face when the threat of cutback disappears. (Diagram 3-5)

DIAGRAM 3—5

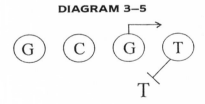

When the guard pulls away, the tackle anchors his outside foot and steps inside and parallel to the line of scrimmage with his inside foot after his initial attack step. He squeezes the center into the opposite-side A gap and crosses his face when the threat of cutback disappears. (Diagram 3-6)

DIAGRAM 3—6

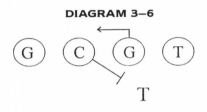

When the guard pulls toward the tackle, the tackle brings his outside foot up and looks for the path of the near back. He looks for a lead or load block by a back or a possible trap block by the other guard. The tackle realizes someone is coming to block him. (Diagram 3-7)

DIAGRAM 3—7

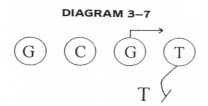

When the near guard steps inside and the opposite guard attempts to trap the tackle, the tackle brings up his outside foot and gets a piece of the guard in an attempt to keep him off the linebacker. He brings his outside foot upfield, turns slightly to face the trapper, and attacks the trapper with his outside shoulder. This is referred to as "wrong arming" the play. It forces the back to bounce to the outside by taking the inside running lane away. This "wrong arming" is a key to the 4-3 Defense since it forces running plays to spill to the outside. (Diagram 3-8)

DIAGRAM 3—8

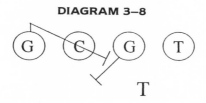

Versus the double-team block, the tackle attacks the offensive tackle with his outside foot and turns his body and falls to his outside knee. At best, he wants to split the double team. At worst, he wants to create a pile and not get moved off or down the line of scrimmage. (Diagram 3-9)

Versus a drop-back pass, the tackle is responsible for the inside rush lane, and he rushes the B gap. On a sprint-out pass, he works one lane wider in the direction of the quarterback.

DIAGRAM 3—9

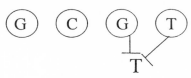

2i alignment

In this alignment, after the tackle reads the helmet of the guard, he feels for the center's block.

The main responsibility of the defensive tackle is to control the A gap versus a run in his direction. On a run away from him, the tackle steps inside and flat with his inside foot. If the center attempts to block him, he squeezes the center into the opposite A gap. By forcing the center into the opposite A gap, the tackle protects his A gap and constricts the opposite A gap. The tackle crosses the face of the center only when the threat of cutback has disappeared, and he then pursues the ball.

Versus a base block, the tackle takes his initial step and follows with his inside foot. He maintains proper leverage and controls the A gap. He squeezes the guard into the B gap and finds the ball. (Diagram 3-10)

DIAGRAM 3—10

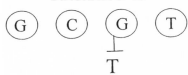

Versus a hook block, the tackle anchors the inside foot and steps outside and parallel to the line of scrimmage with his outside foot, after his initial attack. He maintains inside leverage on the guard as he squeezes him into the B gap. He crosses the face of the guard when the threat of cutback disappears. (Diagram 3-11)

DIAGRAM 3—11

Versus the center–guard fold, the tackle steps inside and parallel to the line of scrimmage with his inside foot. He squeezes the center into the opposite A gap and crosses his face when the threat of cutback disappears. (Diagram 3-12)

DIAGRAM 3–12

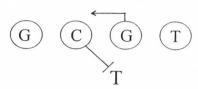

When the guard pulls to the outside, the tackle attempts to get a piece of the guard while sliding his inside foot to the inside. He looks directly to the center. If the center attempts to reach block him, he fights in the direction of the guard pull. If the center blocks to the opposite side, the tackle looks for a trap from the opposite guard. (Diagram 3-13)

DIAGRAM 3–13

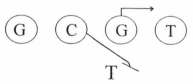

Versus the center–guard double team, the tackle attacks the center with his inside foot and turns his body and falls to his inside knee. At best, he wants to split the double team. At worst, he wants to create a pile and not get moved off or down the line of scrimmage. (Diagram 3-14)

DIAGRAM 3–14

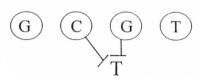

Versus a drop-back pass, the tackle is responsible for the inside rush lane, and he rushes the A gap. On a sprint-out pass, he works one lane wider in the direction of the quarterback.

1 alignment

In this alignment, after the tackle reads the helmet of the center, he feels for the guard's block.

The main responsibility of the defensive tackle is to control the A gap versus a run in his direction. On a run away from him, the tackle squeezes the center into the opposite A gap. From this point, it is the same as the 2i alignment.

Versus the base block, the tackle takes his initial step and follows with his outside foot. He maintains proper leverage and controls the A gap. He squeezes the center into the offside A gap and finds the football. (Diagram 3-15)

DIAGRAM 3—15

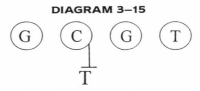

Versus the hook block, the tackle steps parallel to the line of scrimmage with his outside foot. He maintains outside leverage and widens while holding his position on the line of scrimmage. (Diagram 3-16)

DIAGRAM 3—16

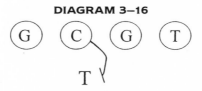

Versus the down block by the guard, the tackle takes his initial step and attacks the center. When he reads the center's attempt to block to the other side, he steps with his outside foot and makes contact with the guard. He fights the pressure of the guard's block and attempts to squeeze him into the B gap. (Diagram 3-17)

DIAGRAM 3—17

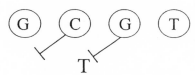

Versus the scoop block, the tackle anchors his outside foot and steps inside and parallel to the line of scrimmage with his inside foot, after his initial attack step. He attempts to keep the center off the linebacker and avoids getting scooped by the guard. (Diagram 3-18)

Versus the double team, the tackle attacks the guard with his outside foot, turns his body, and falls to his outside knee. At best, he wants to split the double team. At worst, he wants to create a pile and not get moved off or down the line of scrimmage. (Diagram 3-19)

Versus the drop-back and sprint-out passes, the tackle uses the same techniques as does the tackle in a 2i alignment.

DIAGRAM 3—18

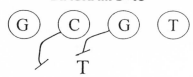

DIAGRAM 3—19

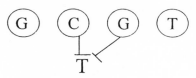

ENDS

Alignments

The strongside defensive tackle employs a 7 alignment on the tight end. (Diagram 3-20)

The weakside defensive tackle employs a 5 alignment on the weakside of the offensive formation.

DIAGRAM 3—20

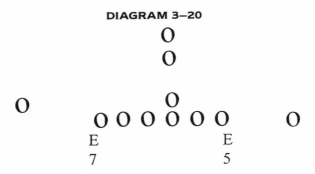

Techniques

The defensive end employs the same techniques as the defensive tackle.

Reads and Reactions Vs.
Various Blocking Schemes

Like the defensive tackles, the defensive ends read the helmet of the offensive player on whom they are aligned as their first key.

7 alignment

In this alignment, after the end reads the helmet of the tight end, he looks to the near back for his next read.

The main responsibility of the defensive end is to maintain outside leverage on the tight end versus a run in his direction. On a run away from him, the end trails the play and checks for a reverse play.

Versus the base block, the end takes his initial step and follows with his outside foot. The end keeps his outside arm and leg free and maintains outside leverage. He squeezes the tight end into the C gap and finds the ball. (Diagram 3-21)

DIAGRAM 3—21

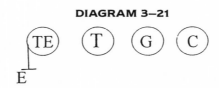

Versus the reach block, the end steps parallel to the line of scrimmage with his outside foot. He works upfield to contain through the outside shoulder of the tight end. He can NEVER get reached! (Diagram 3-22)

DIAGRAM 3—22

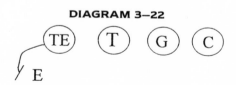

Versus the arc block, the end steps parallel to the line of scrimmage with his outside foot but keeps his inside foot in place. His eyes go immediately back inside to locate the ball. (Diagram 3-23)

DIAGRAM 3—23

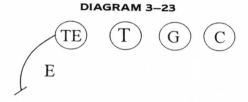

When the tight end steps inside and either guard attempts to trap the end, the end brings up his outside foot and gets his hands on the tight end to flatten his blocking path. He brings his outside foot upfield, turns slightly to face the trapper and attacks the trapper with his outside shoulder. By doing this, he is wrong arming the play. (Diagram 3-24)

Versus the cutoff block, the end anchors his outside foot and steps inside and parallel to the line of scrimmage with his inside foot, after his initial attack step. He squeezes the tight end into the C gap and looks for counter or cutback. (Diagram 3-25)

Versus any pass play, the end is the outside rusher and responsible for outside contain.

DIAGRAM 3—24

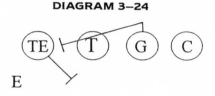

DIAGRAM 3–25

5 alignment

In this alignment, after the end reads the block of the offensive tackle, he looks to the near back for his next read.

The main responsibility of the defensive end is to maintain outside leverage on the offensive tackle versus a run in his direction. On a run away from him, the end trails the play and looks for a reverse or counter play.

The 5 alignment defensive end plays the base, reach, down, and cutoff blocks in the same manner as the 7 alignment defensive end. The 5 alignment defensive end also rushes the passer in the same fashion as the 7 alignment end.

RUSHING THE PASSER

A successful pass rush is an important part of any defensive scheme and an essential part of the 4-3 Defense. As much time must be spent developing proper defensive pass-rushing techniques as is spent by offensive linemen developing pass-blocking techniques.

At Widener University there are several basic pass-rushing fundamentals stressed to the defensive linemen. A defensive lineman must:

1. Anticipate and quickly recognize a passing play.
2. Employ quickness and decisiveness on his initial move.
3. Keep his body leaning forward during the entire rush.
4. Coordinate his hands, feet, and head movements.
5. Never take his eyes off the passer.
6. Attack only one-half of the blocker. This cuts the blocker's effectiveness in half.
7. Get the arms and hands up as he nears the passer.
8. NEVER STOP OR SLOW DOWN!

4

The 4-3 Linebackers

The linebackers, when aligned off the line of scrimmage, employ a balanced two-point stance. The feet are shoulder width apart with the chest over the knees and the weight on the balls of the feet. The middle linebacker keeps his feet parallel, while the outside linebackers drop the outside foot slightly back. This is the basic linebacker stance used in most defenses.

When the linebacker aligns on the line of scrimmage in a 7 alignment, he employs the same stance but drops his outside foot farther back.

When the linebacker is employing a Show and Trick alignment, he aligns in a gap. He is going to either blitz or, at least, trick the quarterback into believing a blitz is coming. He aligns with one foot farther back than the other and looks like a sprinter who is about to explode from a two-point stance.

As explained in Chapter 2, the 4-3 linebackers are more like defensive backs than traditional linebackers. This works very well when all three are off the line of scrimmage in some type of 0 alignment. (Diagram 4-1) However, when an offense makes use of two tight ends, one of the outside linebackers must come up to a 7 alignment and play on a tight end. In the basic 4-3 Defense, it is normally done with the weakside outside linebacker (Will). By changing the alignment of the Will, the weakside tackle can stay in a 1 or 2i alignment, and the weakside end can remain in a 5 alignment. The middle linebacker (Mike) can move his alignment slightly to the weakside and closer to his weakside B gap run responsibility. (Diagram 4-2)

Since the outside linebackers are not as big and strong as the typical outside linebackers, aligning on a tight end in a 7 alignment can cause some mismatch problems. This can certainly be a weakness in the defense. It is extremely important for the outside linebackers to get as

DIAGRAM 4–1

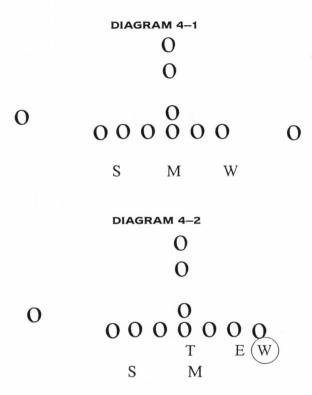

DIAGRAM 4–2

much practice as possible in the 7 alignment. The reads and reactions from this alignment are very similar to those of the defensive end in a 7 alignment (Chapter 3). For this reason, the outside linebackers should spend some time during the practice week with the defensive ends working on the proper techniques in a 7 alignment.

MIDDLE LINEBACKER (MIKE)

Alignments

The Mike may align from 20i to 20i. He normally aligns midway between the two gaps he is responsible for versus the run (strongside A Gap and weakside B Gap). This alignment varies with the offensive formation and the game plan. As a starting point, the depth of the Mike is five yards from the line of scrimmage. This also may vary with various down-and-distance situations. (Diagram 4-3)

DIAGRAM 4–3

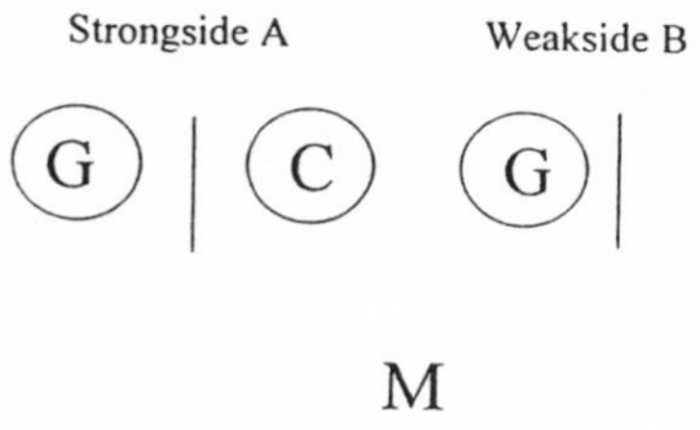

Strongside A   Weakside B

$$\text{G} \mid \text{C} \quad \text{G} \mid$$

M

Techniques

The Mike makes all strength calls for the front. His first job is to recognize the offensive formation and make the proper call. Without a Mike who has the ability to handle this extremely important job, the 4-3 Defense could be in serious trouble.

The Mike employs a hand shiver when he attacks blockers. He does not go around blocks but through them. Like the defensive linemen, the Mike protects his gap while pushing any blocker into the next onside (to the side of the running play) gap. Since he does not have to worry about cutback, he has much more freedom to cross the face of the blocker to get to the ballcarrier than do the defensive linemen. If a gap opens, the Mike is allowed to shoot it to make the play in the backfield. However, he can never go "back door" (around the backside of the blocker, instead of through his face), unless he is SURE he can make the tackle. (Diagram 4-4) Using the back-door technique can allow the Mike to get cut off, and if this happens, a big offensive play can be the result. (Diagram 4-4)

DIAGRAM 4–4

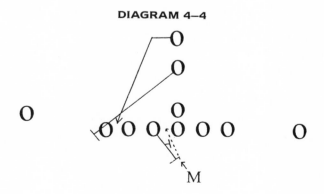

M

Reads and Reactions

The Mike is responsible for the strongside A gap and the weakside B gap versus the run and is known as a "downhill" player. Downhill refers to the Mike's job of stepping up and attacking the line of scrimmage to stop the inside running game. He is not responsible for getting to the outside but is responsible for tackling every inside running play. He must react up now!

He keys the near running back to the far running back and then the blocking scheme. However, this rather extensive key-reading process has been simplified by lessening the need to thoroughly read the blocking scheme. This can be accomplished by reading the "spot" after the initial backfield read.

The spot is an imaginary circle on the ground directly below the tail of the offensive center. Once the Mike makes his initial step in the direction of the backfield key and toward the line of scrimmage, with peripheral vision he keeps an eye on the spot. When an offensive player crosses the spot opposite the direction of the initial backfield key, the Mike recognizes a counter play and works back toward the spot and, therefore, the running play. In many 4-3 defensive schemes, the Mike is often lost versus a counter trap play. Using the spot read, Mike sees the offensive trapper (guard, tackle, tight end, or back) cross the spot and he reacts to this movement. Reading the spot is simple to teach and learn and is extremely effective. Reading the spot also reduces the amount of practice time required for the Mike to read the various blocking schemes he will face in a particular game.

When the Mike reads pass, he either drops into the appropriate zone or covers the man he has been assigned to cover. This is determined by the coverage being employed. This is covered in more detail in Chapter 7.

OUTSIDE LINEBACKERS
(WEAKSIDE—WILL; STRONGSIDE—SAM)

Note: This description of the outside linebackers describes both the weakside and strongside positions. When one facet of the description covers both positions (Will and Sam), only one explanation is used. When a facet of the description is different for each position, two explanations are employed.

Alignments

The Sam aligns in a 50 alignment. The Will aligns in a 50 alignment when there is an open end and no slot to his side. (Diagram 4-5) However, when the 4-3 Defense faces an offense with two tight ends, the Will aligns in a 7 alignment. (Diagram 4-6)

When aligned in a 50 alignment, the depth of the outside linebackers is five yards from the line of scrimmage. This may vary with down-and-distance situations.

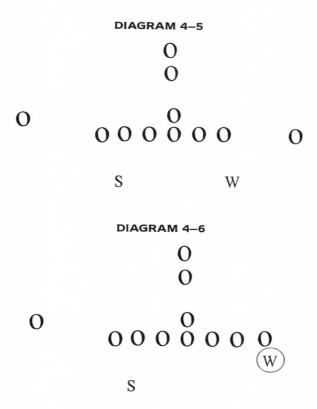

DIAGRAM 4-5

DIAGRAM 4-6

Techniques

All outside linebackers are taught to play the weakside and strongside positions. They are taught the techniques required to play both the Sam and Will linebackers. This eliminates two possible problems.

There is a need for only three good outside linebackers when entering a game; if either starter is injured, the reserve can go in as a capable substitute. If there are outside linebackers who play only the Sam or the Will position, there is a need to have four good outside linebackers ready for a game, one reserve for each position.

There are also offensive teams who stem the tight end (switch the tight end from one side of the offensive formation to the other side) prior to the start of a play. It is impractical to have the Sam switch with the Will versus this offensive maneuver. If the defensive personnel switched with each offensive change of strength, it would be playing into the hands of the offense by allowing the offense to manipulate the defense.

The ability of one player to play both the Sam and the Will positions allows the defensive coach a great deal of flexibility. Depending on the strengths of the opponent, the 4-3 defensive coach can employ a right and left outside linebacker or a strongside and weakside linebacker. This is particularly effective against a team with a strong tendency to run to one side more than the other. It allows the defensive coach to put his strongest outside linebacker to the side where most runs are expected. The practice of teaching players to master the weakside and strongside techniques is employed not only for the outside linebackers but for every position in the 4-3 Defense at Widener University (except the Mike, of course).

Like the Mike, the outside linebackers employ the hand shiver versus an offensive blocker. However, unlike the Mike, they do cross the face of the blocker to get to the ball.

Reads and Reactions

The Sam is responsible for the strongside C gap. The Will, when aligned in a 50 alignment, is responsible for both the weakside B Gap and the weakside D Gap. The Will is responsible for the weakside B Gap when two running backs enter that gap. When this occurs, the Will keeps outside leverage on the weakside B Gap, and the Mike takes inside leverage on the weakside B Gap. This prevents a team from running an isolation play (Diagram 4-7) or a lead-belly play into the weakside B gap. (Diagram 4-8) Versus either play, if the Will does not check the B gap before going to the D gap, there is the strong possibility the lead blocker can pin the Mike inside, and this leaves no defender in a position to take the running back breaking to the outside of the B gap.

Versus a double tight-end set, the Will aligns in a 7 alignment and is responsible for the weakside D gap or outside contain.

DIAGRAM 4—7

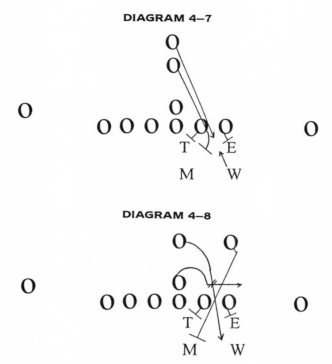

DIAGRAM 4—8

The outside linebackers are not downhill players. They shuffle parallel to the line of scrimmage until a blocker attacks them. They step up to make a tackle or to attack the player who is about to block them.

The outside linebackers key the near offensive running back to the far offensive running back and then the blocking scheme. Versus any set with two backs in the backfield, not in an I-formation, the primary key for the outside linebackers is the back to their side. When that back goes away, they look to the opposite back for a counter play or cutback.

Since the outside linebackers do not attack downhill, the onside (to the side of the running play) outside linebacker is expected to chase down any running play that is spilled to the outside.

The offside (to the side away from the running play) outside linebacker reacts to a run going away from him by becoming the "hitman." The hitman is responsible for the cutback play. Rather than flying to the onside, the hitman keeps his depth and shuffles toward the onside, looking for any cutback or counter play. The Will also plays the hitman from the 7 alignment. He drops off the ball and gains depth when his key goes away.

DIAGRAM 4—9

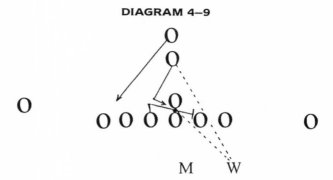

Like the Mike, the offside outside linebackers are coached to see the spot. When their key goes away, they look directly at the spot to see if any offensive player is crossing it. This spot read helps greatly in stopping the counter game. (Diagram 4-9)

When the outside linebackers read pass, they either drop into the appropriate zone or cover the man who has been assigned to them. This is determined by the coverage being employed. This is covered in more detail in Chapter 7.

5

The 4-3 Secondary
in Cover 2 (Blue Spot)

In the preceding chapters involving the 4-3 defensive front, the Basic 40 Front was used, and all position descriptions dealt with that particular front. For this chapter, a particular coverage had to be chosen to describe the basic positions of safety and corner. Cover 2, or Blue Spot as it is named at Widener University, is the coverage selected. Blue Spot is very similar to most common forms of Cover 2, but it has several unique differences. This coverage was selected because the preliminary alignment for Blue Spot is the starting point for many different coverages.

Many people think of the 4-3 Defense as a seven-man front with a two-deep zone secondary. Although the two-deep zone secondary is one of the coverages employed, it is not necessarily the coverage most often employed. However, the initial alignment of the two-deep secondary is the most-often-used pre-snap alignment. At Widener University, we often align in the two-deep zone coverage look and employ another coverage on the snap of the ball. It is referred to as aligning in a two-deep "shell." This alignment is employed as a disguise and to prevent the quarterback from making the correct pre-snap coverage read. In Chapter 7, all other coverages are described, and their relationship to the two-deep shell is discussed.

As in all defenses, the secondary is the most crucial segment of the starting defensive eleven. This unit is considered the most crucial because they can least afford to make an error. When a member of the defensive front makes an error, the result could be a ten- or fifteen-yard gain by the offense. When a member of the secondary unit makes a coverage error, the result may be an opponent touchdown. For defensive success, and ultimately team success, the secondary has to be that segment of the defensive team that makes the least number of errors.

The defensive backs employ a two-point stance with the feet slightly less than shoulder width apart. The chest is over the knees but not quite as far over as it is for the linebackers. The corners align with the inside foot just behind the outside foot and the entire body cocked slightly to the inside to get a good view of the backfield. The safeties align with the outside foot just behind the inside foot, with shoulders parallel to the line of scrimmage. In a zone coverage, prior to the snap of the ball, the defensive backs are coached to analyze the offensive formation to determine who may be a possible pass-receiving threat to their area of responsibility. This technique keeps the secondary alert and rarely off guard. Through the practice week, the secondary reviews the formations and plays of opponents and learns what to expect from each offensive formation in every possible down-and-distance situation.

SAFETIES

As explained in Chapter 2, it is beneficial to have two safeties who are interchangeable. The strong safety can play the free safety position and vice versa. This is particularly true when Blue Spot is used. In essence, this coverage requires two free safeties, rather than a free safety and a strong safety.

Alignments

The safety aligns midway between the alignments of the offensive number one and number two. However, the safety never aligns more than five yards inside the hash mark to the sideline. It is important to remember that hash marks are different for high school and college. The alignment rules of the safety apply to the college hash marks.

There are those proponents of the 4-3 Defense who align according to the hash marks and pay little attention to the offensive formation. In Cover 2, the safety is generally responsible for the deep patterns run by number one and/or number two to his side. How could there be a better starting position than midway between those two players? At Widener University, we are much more interested in the offensive formation than in the hash marks when Cover 2 (Blue Spot) is employed.

The depth of the safety is between twelve and fifteen yards. This is determined by the speed of the offensive receivers and the patterns they employ in various down-and-distance situations. (Diagram 5-1)

DIAGRAM 5–1

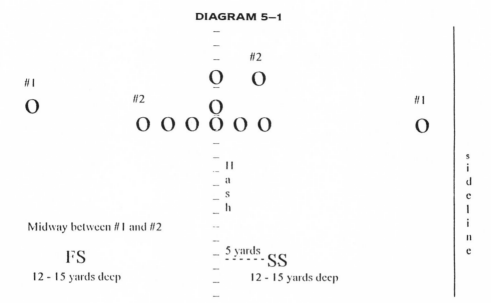

Techniques

In Blue Spot, the safety may be a zone player or a man-to-man defender, depending on the patterns of number two. On the snap of the ball, the safety begins to walk backward in a slow, deliberate style. This walk is the first phase of the backpedal. The walk should last for at least three steps. During this walk, the safety is reading his keys to determine run or pass.

When a pass play is read, the safety continues to move backward but in a jog, rather than a walk. During this phase of the backpedal, the safety is analyzing the patterns. If a deep pattern is read by the safety, the jog becomes a backward run. When the receiver nears the safety, the safety turns and runs with the receiver, keeping enough of a cushion to prevent himself from getting beaten deep. On all deep patterns, the safety plays the upfield shoulder of the receiver. In this way, the safety should be able to stay deeper than the receiver.

When the safety reads a running play and is sure there is no threat of a pass (*Remember: The safety is a pass defender first and a run defender second in this coverage*), he reads the movement of the corner to his side. When the corner attacks the play to the inside, the safety comes up, under control, to the outside. When the corner remains outside, the safety comes up, under control, to the inside. When the ball is run away

DIAGRAM 5—2

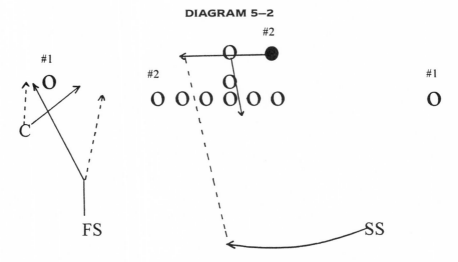

from the safety, he rotates through the deep middle zone. The safety stays on the inside hip of the ballcarrier and prevents any deep cutback. (Diagram 5-2)

Reads and Reactions

The safety keys the quarterback to number two. When the safety recognizes a pass play, he immediately reads the pattern of number two. When number two executes a vertical pattern, or a deep-inside pattern, the safety covers number two with man-to-man coverage. After number two has gotten ten yards downfield, it is considered a vertical pattern,

DIAGRAM 5—3

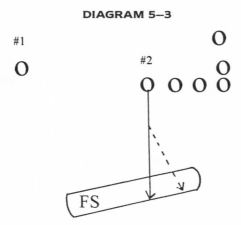

and the safety must cover it. However, he does not have to rush up to pick up number two because he is being undercovered by a linebacker. (Diagram 5-3)

When number two executes a horizontal release, the safety looks for the vertical pattern by number one and covers that pattern with man-to-man coverage. (Diagram 5-4)

When number two does not release or runs a short inside pattern, the safety falls to the deep middle area and plays as a true zone free safety. (Diagram 5-5)

DIAGRAM 5—4

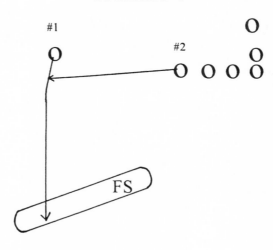

DIAGRAM 5—5

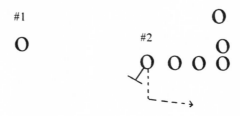

CORNERS

Alignments

The corner aligns six yards deep and one yard outside of number one. This is known as a "squat" alignment. (Diagram 5-6) There are times when the corners will initially align in a "lock" alignment on number two, prior to the snap of the ball. In the lock alignment, the corner aligns with his nose on the outside shoulder of number one, as close to the line of scrimmage as possible. When Blue Spot is being used, the lock alignment is a disguise. It is hoped the quarterback will make a pre-snap read and believe the coverage is a two-deep man-to-man coverage, rather than a two-deep zone coverage. Prior to the snap of the ball, the corner relocates to his squat alignment and plays from there. (Diagram 5-7)

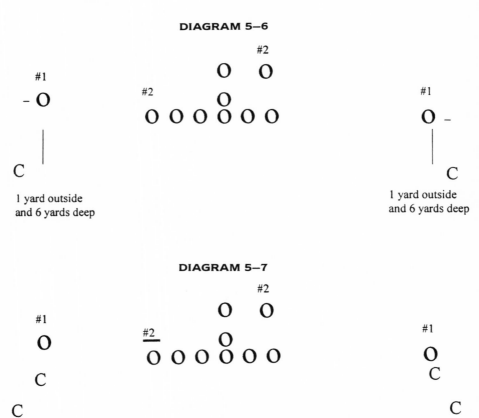

DIAGRAM 5—6

1 yard outside
and 6 yards deep

1 yard outside
and 6 yards deep

DIAGRAM 5—7

Techniques

The corner is responsible for disrupting the pattern of number one. On the snap of the ball, the corner holds his position and does not backpedal. He waits to make contact with number one. The only movement the corner makes is to slide out or in, parallel to the line of scrimmage, with the release of number one. The corner keeps his inside shoulder on the outside shoulder of number one. The corner's goal is to disrupt the pattern of number one.

The corner's technique used to be referred to as a "funnel" technique. The corner was expected to make contact with number one and force him to the inside. This was done to prevent number one from running a fade pattern and beating the safety to the deep outside zone. (Diagram 5-8) However, offensive coaches realized what was happening and instructed number one to make a wide outside release and put the corner in a difficult position to funnel him. The defensive remedy is to slide with number one and force him to go as wide as possible. By forcing number one to go wide, the goal of keeping the receiver from beating the safety in the deep outside zone is still accomplished. While executing this technique, the corner maintains his six yards' depth and still looks inside to read the pattern of number two.

DIAGRAM 5—8

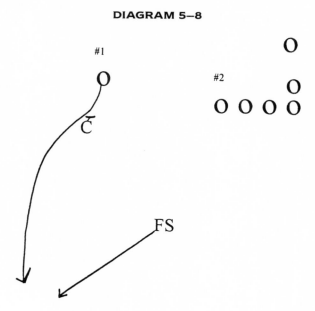

Reads and Reactions

The corner keys through number one to number two. When number two executes a vertical release, releases inside, or blocks, the corner covers number one with man-to-man coverage. (Diagram 5-9)

When number two releases horizontally, the corner disrupts the pattern of number one and drops to a depth of twelve yards. From this depth, the corner can come up on a pass to number two. (Diagram 5-10)

The corner is in a good position to discourage a pass to number one in the "soft area" or, at least, to force a pass over his outstretched arms to number one. The soft area is the vacuum between the safety (who is running to cover number one) and behind the corner. By dropping to a depth of twelve yards, the corner shrinks this area and helps make a completion to number one very difficult. (Diagram 5-11)

At the twelve-yard depth, the corner is also in a good position to cover the wheel pattern. As number two turns upfield, the corner picks up number two and covers him with man-to-man coverage. (Diagram 5-12)

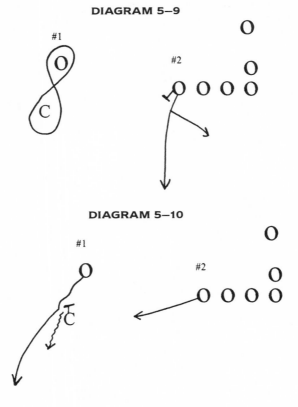

DIAGRAM 5—9

DIAGRAM 5—10

DIAGRAM 5–11

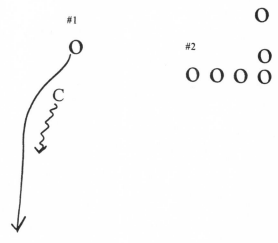

DIAGRAM 5–12

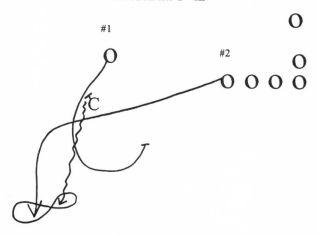

GENERAL TECHNIQUES FOR THE
SECONDARY IN THE 4-3 DEFENSE

The following are techniques employed by the defensive backs at Widener University. Although these techniques apply to most defensive schemes, they are critical to a successful secondary in the 4-3 Defense.

Zone Coverages

1. The DB analyzes the offensive formation prior to the snap of the ball. This allows the DB to recognize all possible threats to his area of responsibility (zone).
2. The DB never "covers grass." When there is no receiver in his zone and/or no threat of a receiver coming into his zone, the DB goes to help cover the nearest receiver.
3. The DB covers the deepest receiver in his zone. It is much simpler to break up on a pass to a shallow receiver than it is to break back on a pass to a deep receiver.
4. Once the pass play is recognized, the DB reads through the receiver in his zone to the quarterback. When the quarterback takes his non-throwing hand off the ball, the DB begins to break in the direction the quarterback is facing.
5. The DB breaks in front of the receiver on all patterns thrown in front of him (out, in, slants, hooks, curls, etc.) to make the interception. He plays over the top of all deep patterns (downfield shoulder of the receiver) to prevent a deep completion and to intercept all deep patterns (fade, fly, post, flag, etc.).

Man to Man

1. The DB plays on the inside of the receiver he is covering. He establishes a position between the receiver and the quarterback on all short patterns. On deep patterns, he maintains the inside position but plays on the downfield shoulder of the receiver to prevent a deep completion.
2. The DB plays in a very physical manner and tries to collide with the receiver and knock the receiver off his route.
3. If beaten deep, the DB does not look for the ball but sprints to catch the receiver.

Part II

Front and Secondary Variations

Every defensive system employs front and secondary variations. The 4-3 Defense is certainly no exception to this rule. The most important thing about variations, for all defensive systems, is to know when and why to employ the variation, as well as the base defense, and to understand the strengths and weaknesses of each. To employ defensive variations without knowing the when, why, strengths, and weaknesses is certainly not sound defensive thinking.

In this section of the book, many variations are covered. The reasons for their use, as well as the strengths and weaknesses of each variation, are discussed. Widener University employs many of the same variations used by the University of Miami and the Dallas Cowboys. However, some of the reasons for employing these variations may differ.

One of the most common reasons for employing a defensive variation is to present another look to an offensive team in order to cause some confusion or indecision on the part of the offensive personnel. All defensive teams, at one time or another, use variations for this purpose. Although this is one reason for the use of some defensive variations at Widener University, more specific reasons are discussed in this section of the book.

6

4-3 Front Variations and Line Stunts

Prior to a discussion of the front variations, it is important to understand why the weakside tackle, in the Base Front, makes use of a 1 and a 2i alignment.

By far, the most common alignment for the weakside tackle is the 1 alignment. In the 1 alignment, normally, the center is forced to block the weakside tackle, and this eliminates the center as a blocker on the Mike. This is particularly true on a running play to the strongside. Due to the 1 alignment, it is very difficult for the weakside offensive guard to scoop block the weakside defensive tackle and keep him from getting involved in defending against the running play. This forces the center to block the tackle in the 1 alignment, and the center cannot be used to block the Mike. This is a definite strength of the 1 alignment. (Diagram 6-1)

DIAGRAM 6—1

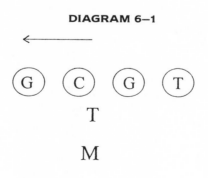

When an offensive team makes use of a weakside running game, particularly any play run in the B gap with a back as a lead blocker, the 2i alignment is much more effective than the 1 alignment. In a 1 alignment, the weakside offensive guard has a great angle to block the weakside tackle and create a large seam for the Mike and Will to cover. (Diagram 6-2) The weakside defensive tackle, aligned in a 2i, cuts down the size of the seam and gives the Mike and the Will a smaller B gap to control. (Diagram 6-3)

At Widener University, it is rare to find the weakside tackle in a 2i alignment. The 1 alignment is, by far, the most common alignment for the weakside tackle. The Mike and the Will are expected to cover the weakside B gap on any isolation or lead-block play.

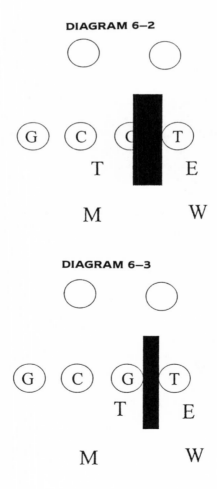

DIAGRAM 6–2

DIAGRAM 6–3

FRONT VARIATIONS

There are numerous front variations in the 4-3 Defense. There could be a separate book written on just these variations. This chapter covers the most commonly used variations.

Flop (Diagram 6-4)

The difference between the Flop Front and the Base Front involves the alignment of the strongside end and the Sam linebacker. The strongside end moves to a 5 alignment and the Sam moves to a 7 alignment. All other members of the front remain in the Base Front alignment.

DIAGRAM 6—4

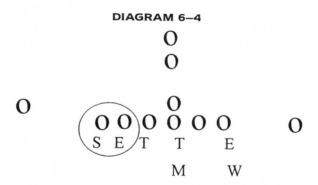

One reason for using the Flop is to be stronger against a strongside running attack. By putting three defenders, instead of two, on the line of scrimmage, a more solid defensive front is presented, and this makes it more difficult to execute a successful running play.

Flop also forces the offensive tackle to play across from a much bigger and stronger athlete than the Sam linebacker, the player he faces in the Base Front. This can cause some blocking problems for the offensive tackle.

A definite weakness of the Flop Front occurs when facing a running play to the weakside. The Sam, in a 7 alignment, has difficulty becoming the hitman. He has to recognize a run to the weakside and then drop off the ball and toward the onside to stop the cutback. In the Base Front, he is in a much better position to stop the cutback. (Diagram 6-5)

DIAGRAM 6–5

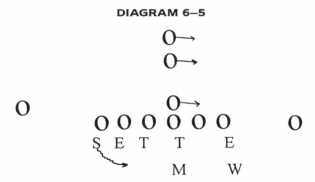

At Widener, versus a double-tight-end offense, the Flop Front is not used. When the Flop Front is called in the defensive huddle and the double-tight-end offense is employed, the Mike checks to (changes to) the Base Front. If the check is not called, the defense ends up with only the Mike off the line of scrimmage. (Diagram 6-6) It is much preferred for pursuit and hitman reasons to have, at least, one of the two outside linebackers off the line of scrimmage. Remember, the outside line-backers are expected to stop all outside runs before they turn upfield. It is a much more difficult task to do this from an on-the-line alignment than from an off-the-line alignment.

DIAGRAM 6–6

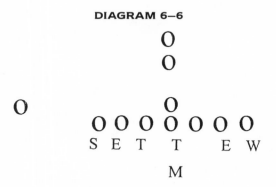

Weak (Diagram 6-7)

The Weak Front is a mirror image of the Base Front. The strongside personnel (the Sam, strongside end, and strongside tackle) align to the strongside of the offensive formation but use weakside alignment rules. The weakside personnel (the Will, weakside end, and weakside tackle) align to the weakside of the offensive formation but use strongside alignment rules. As discussed in Chapter 1, for the front the strongside is the side of the offensive formation with the tight end. Since all members of the defense (except the Mike) learn to play both the weakside and strongside position, it is very simple to get into this front.

The Weak Front possesses the same strengths and weaknesses as the Base Front. However, used versus certain offensive formations and plays, it is an extremely effective front.

When an offense employs a single-tight-end formation and attacks the defense with a weakside running attack, the Weak Front can be an effective defensive tool in stopping the running game. The Weak Front possesses the same run-stopping advantages to the weakside as the Flop Front possesses to the strongside, with one additional advantage. The Weak Front allows the Will to play off the ball, unlike the Sam in the Flop Front. This puts the Will in a better position to cover an onside outside play.

Being off the ball, in the Weak Front, affords the Will several more advantages over the Sam, aligned in the Flop Front. The Will is in a much better position to become the hitman and, because of his depth, is in a better position to get into pass coverage. Being a pass defender from a 7 alignment is not a simple task, and this is one reason the Flop Front is not used a great deal in a passing situation. The Weak Front also puts the Will in a good situation from which to blitz (covered in depth in Chapter 8).

When an offensive team employs a double-tight-end offense, some of the advantages of the Weak Front disappear. The front merely becomes a Base Front, with the weakside and the strongside personnel exchanging alignments. There are few advantages to playing the front in this manner. Normally, at Widener University, the Mike checks to the Base Front, allowing the front defenders to play their normal alignments.

DIAGRAM 6–7

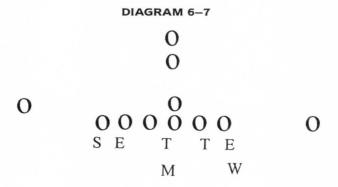

Both the Flop and Weak fronts are often employed to cause a mismatch between an offensive lineman and a defensive lineman. This is particularly true when a pass play is expected. The defensive coach, from scouting reports or game films, may discover a weakness in a particular offensive lineman and employ either the Flop Front or Weak Front to put a superior defender on an inferior blocker.

Like the Base Front, both the Flop Front and the Weak Front are employed in nearly all down-and-distance situations and are effective versus both running and passing plays.

Loose (Diagram 6-8)

The Loose Front is somewhat unique even though there are similarities between it and the Flop Front or Weak Front. Unlike fronts already discussed, the Loose Front is employed in a particular down-and-distance situation. It is used when the offense is expected to pass. Depending on the offensive formation employed, it is not nearly as strong against the running game as are the previously analyzed fronts.

The alignments of the strongside end and the Sam are different than those of the Base Front, Flop Front, or the Weak Front. Depending on the offensive formation employed to the weakside, the alignment of the weakside end is also different than those alignments already discussed.

Versus a tight-end set, the strongside end uses a 9 alignment and cocks slightly to the inside. On the snap of the ball, he aims at a point directly behind the tight end and explodes toward that point as he reads the movement of the tight end. The main job of the ends in a Loose Front is to rush the passer. However, if the tight end attempts to block out on him, the defensive end jams the tight end back to the inside and locates the ball.

DIAGRAM 6—8

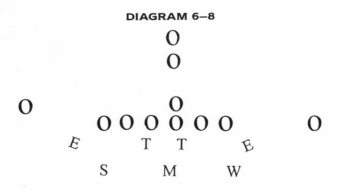

When the strongside end aligns against an offense with no tight end, he employs a 7 alignment and uses the same techniques against the offensive tackle that he uses versus the tight end. The weakside defensive end uses the same alignments and techniques used by the strongside end versus the offensive tackle. (Diagram 6-9)

DIAGRAM 6—9

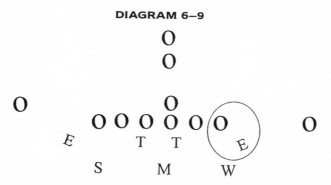

The Sam, versus a tight end, uses a 60 alignment and keys through the tight end to the near back. The Sam is thinking pass but must react up to an out block by the tight end on the strongside defensive end. This block indicates run and the Sam must fill the C gap. (Diagram 6-10) Versus a formation with no tight end, the Sam employs his basic 50 alignment and steps up only if the offensive tackle attempts an out block on the defensive end. (Diagram 6-11) The Will uses the same alignments and techniques used by the Sam versus an offensive tackle.

DIAGRAM 6—10

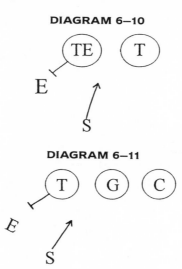

DIAGRAM 6—11

Unlike the Base Front, the Flop Front, and the Weak Front, the Loose Front may be used to both sides of the defensive front or to one side only. When it is to be employed by the entire front, "Loose" is called as the front call. When the Loose Front is employed to only one side, the other side uses the Base Front alignment. An example of a huddle call using the Loose Front to one side is "Loose Strong"— followed by a secondary call. (Diagram 6-12) It may also be called as "Loose Weak." (Diagram 6-13)

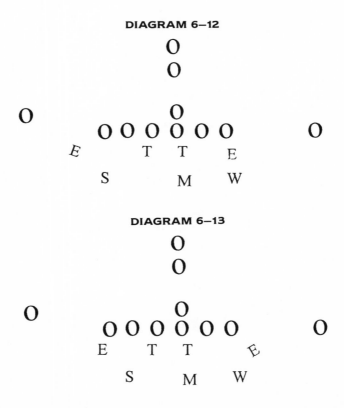

DIAGRAM 6–12

DIAGRAM 6–13

When the Loose Front is employed to both sides, like the Basic Front, an adjustment must be made versus an offense with a tight end to both sides. Like the Base front, the adjustment is made to the weakside, and it is the same adjustment as the Base Front adjustment. (Diagram 6-14)

Although the Loose Front is designed for an excellent pass rush by the defensive ends, it can be used effectively versus the running game. It presents an excellent change of pace to an offense that has become accustomed to seeing the fronts previously presented in this chapter.

DIAGRAM 6–14

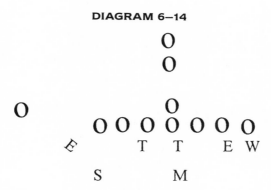

LINE STUNTS

The stunts described in this chapter involve at least two of the four down defensive linemen and may involve all four. These stunts may be employed versus the running or passing game with equal effectiveness.

Stem

This stunt involves initially aligning in one front and moving to the designated huddle call prior to the snap of the ball. It could involve the entire defensive front or several members of the defensive front. Those involved with the stunt initially align in the front that is opposite the designated huddle call.

When no position follows the Stem call, the entire defensive front employs the stunt. An example of this call in the huddle is "40 Weak–Stem–..." followed by a secondary call. Since the opposite of a Weak Front is a Base Front, the defensive front aligns in a Base Front and, prior to the snap of the ball, moves to a Weak Front. Versus an offensive formation with a tight end to the strongside and a split end to the weakside, the movements are as follows:

- Strongside End—From a 7 alignment to a 5 alignment
- Sam—From a 50 alignment to a 7 alignment
- Strongside Tackle—From a 3 alignment to a 1 alignment
- Mike—No change
- Weakside Tackle—From a 1 alignment to a 3 alignment

- Will—No change
- Weakside End—No change (Diagram 6-15)

When a position (or positions) follows the Stem Call, only those players named execute the Stem. An example of this call in the huddle is "40 Flop–End and Sam Stem–..." followed by a secondary call. Since the opposite of the Flop Front is a Base Front, the strongside end and the Sam align in a Base Front and, prior to the snap of the ball, move to the Flop Front. Versus an offensive formation with a tight end to the strongside and a split end to the weakside, the movements are as follows:

- Strongside End—From a 7 alignment to a 5 alignment
- Sam—From a 50 alignment to a 7 alignment (Diagram 6-16)

DIAGRAM 6–15

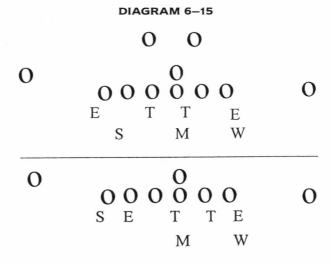

There are numerous possibilities for the use of the stunt. It is strictly up to the creativity of the defensive coach.

The Stem is used to create confusion in the offensive blocking scheme and can give the defense a great advantage. However, when the ball is snapped, prior to or during the Stem, defensive problems can result. In order to eliminate problems, the stunt should not be used too frequently. When the offense recognizes a pattern in the use of this stunt, they merely go on a quick count, and this neutralizes the effectiveness of the stunt.

DIAGRAM 6—16

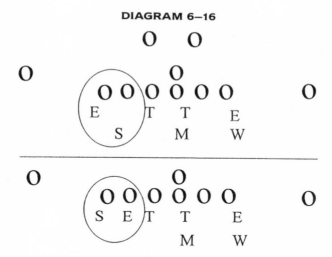

Texas

This is a stunt involving the defensive tackle and defensive end, and it is used as a means of getting an effective pass rush. It is most effective when the tackle is employing a 3 alignment, and the end is in a 5 alignment. On recognizing a pass play, both defensive linemen begin their pass rush. The end steps to the middle of the offensive tackle and makes contact. After the initial contact, the end takes a hard inside charge. The tackle maintains contact with the guard long enough to keep him from picking up the defensive end. The tackle then steps to the outside and rushes the C gap. (Diagram 6-17)

Having the defensive tackle occupy the guard could give the defensive end a free rush to the quarterback, if he can beat the offensive tackle with a good inside move. However, the best chance for a sack comes from the defensive tackle. Since the defensive tackle maintains contact with the guard, the guard should commit to blocking him or, at worst, should step to the defensive end. The offensive tackle should attempt to prevent the inside rush by the defensive end, and this opens up the outside and allows the tackle a great rushing lane to the quarterback.

DIAGRAM 6—17

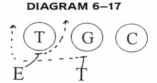

The key to this stunt is how effectively the defensive linemen convince the offensive lineman to expect a normal straight pass rush. Contact is the most important aspect of this stunt. Both defensive linemen cannot be in too big of a hurry to get into the stunt, especially the tackle. When the timing is correct, this stunt provides an excellent pass rush.

The Texas Stunt is unsuccessful when the defensive linemen execute it too quickly. The offensive linemen read the stunt, the guard picks up the defensive end and the offensive tackle picks up the defensive tackle. (Diagram 6-18)

DIAGRAM 6–18

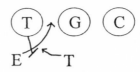

Ed It and Tom It

Like the Texas Stunt, the Ed It and Tom It stunts involve the defensive tackle and the defensive end. They also are most effectively executed when the end employs a 5 alignment and the tackle uses a 3 alignment. These stunts can be used in a passing situation to get a more effective pass rush but are most effective versus the running game. In both stunts, one of the defensive linemen uses a gap charge, while the other employs a loop charge. In both stunts, the two defensive linemen exchange gap responsibilities.

When the Ed It Stunt is employed, the defensive end must tighten his 5 alignment. He should get as close as nose on nose with the offensive tackle without alerting the tackle to the upcoming stunt. On the snap of the ball, the defensive end executes a gap charge into the B gap and looks to the guard as his key. The defensive end avoids contact with the guard and looks for penetration into the backfield. The end executes this move with reckless abandon and attempts "to make something happen." If the guard attempts to block the defensive end, the end uses his normal rule of pushing the offensive lineman into the next gap (A gap). Using this technique, the defensive end protects his gap (B gap) and collapses the A gap.

On the snap of the ball, the defensive tackle takes a step with his outside foot, parallel to the line of scrimmage. He keeps his shoulders square and attacks the C gap while looking to the offensive tackle as his key. If the offensive tackle attempts to block the defensive tackle, the defensive tackle goes against his normal rule of pushing the offensive tackle into gap. Instead, the defensive tackle immediately fights across the face of the offensive tackle. He must get to the C gap and cannot allow himself to be blocked inside by the offensive tackle. If the offensive tackle blocks the defensive tackle to the inside, the defense is left with two B gap players (defensive tackle and defensive end) and no C gap player. (Diagram 6-18)

The Tom It Stunt is the opposite of the Ed It Stunt. The defensive tackle executes the gap charge through the B gap, while the defensive end executes the loop charge to the A gap. The defensive tackle must, again, tighten his 5 alignment to prevent himself from being blocked outside by the guard. (Diagram 6-19)

DIAGRAM 6—19

While these two stunts can cause numerous blocking problems for the offense, they have one major weakness. If the defensive lineman, executing the loop charge, gets cut off, a gap is left undefended. This could easily cause a major problem for the defense. As with the Texas Stunt, the defensive coach must pick the right time to use the Ed It or Tom It stunts and not use either of them too frequently.

7

4-3 Secondary Variations

Prior to a discussion of secondary variations, it is necessary to understand how the secondary coverages are called in the huddle at Widener University.

MAKING THE SECONDARY CALLS
IN THE HUDDLE

There are three ways the coverages can be called. A single coverage can be called, and it is to be used no matter what offensive formation is employed. This is normally the case when a blitz is being used and a form of man-to-man coverage is employed (Pink or Red coverage).

The second method is to call two coverages in the huddle. One of the coverages is for one or more particular offensive formations. The second coverage is to be used against any other formation employed by the offense.

The third method is to call "Match" in the defensive huddle. Match means to match particular coverages to particular formations. This, like all other coverage calls, is based on the scouting report of the opponent. Perhaps Blue Spot is to be employed against a pro set and Green Spot versus a double-split-end set and Orange versus a double-wing set. Against all other formations, Silver is to be used. The Match call is certainly the most common call.

Variations

Many proponents of the 4-3 Defense use the five-under, two-deep zone (Cover 2) as their primary zone-pass coverage. At Widener University, although Cover 2 (Blue Spot) is not necessarily the most-used coverage, the Blue Spot alignment is the starting point for many other coverages, and it is often employed as a disguise. There are also situations where the basic alignments of other coverages are used as disguises, prior to the snap of the ball.

Along with the secondary descriptions, this chapter also includes basic descriptions of the responsibilities of the linebackers versus the pass.

ZONE COVERAGES

The coverages described in this section are classified as zone coverages. However, there are situations in Blue Spot when certain secondary players employ man-to-man coverage within the zone coverage being used (Chapter 5).

Blue Spot (Cover 2)

Blue Spot was thoroughly covered in Chapter 5 as far as the secondary players are concerned. However, the play of the linebackers was not covered. The linebackers' zone-pass responsibilities in Blue Spot are the starting point for all other coverages. The linebackers are first taught their zone-coverage responsibilities in Blue Spot, and all other coverages evolve from these.

Like the secondary players, the linebackers are expected to analyze the offensive formation, prior to the snap of the ball, and to determine which receivers could possibly threaten the zone for which they are responsible. This pre-snap read is very important and helps lead to excellent pass coverage.

The outside linebacker's responsibility in Blue Spot is simply referred to as "Curl," and the linebacker knows the responsibilities of the safeties and corners as far as reading the release of #2 is concerned.

When the offense employs a wide receiver (#1) with no #2 on or near the line of scrimmage, the outside linebacker recognizes the wide receiver as a possible threat to the Curl zone. Since there is no #2, the outside linebacker knows that the corner is covering the wide receiver with man-to-man coverage. However, this has little effect on the outside linebacker's pass coverage. The outside linebacker realizes a #2 could slip out of the backfield, and the corner would pick up #2 and leave #1. With this in mind, on recognition of pass, the outside linebacker drops toward the wide receiver with his head on a swivel. He looks from the wide receiver to the quarterback and makes sure there is no draw play. (Diagram 7-1)

DIAGRAM 7–1

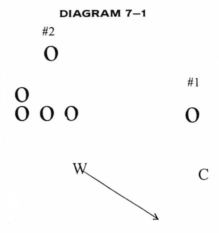

When the wide receiver executes a Curl pattern, the linebacker hangs inside the wide receiver, between the wide receiver and the quarterback. By hanging inside the wide receiver, the linebacker is forcing a longer throw by the quarterback. (Diagram 7-2)

DIAGRAM 7–2

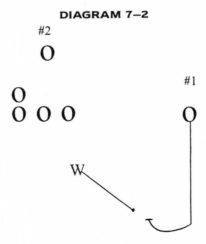

When the wide receiver executes an out pattern, the linebacker sprints to get under the out pattern. He forces the quarterback to throw over him. (Diagram 7-3)

When the wide receiver executes a deep pattern (over sixteen yards), the linebacker continues to drop, looking for an underneath pattern. (Diagram 7-4)

DIAGRAM 7—3

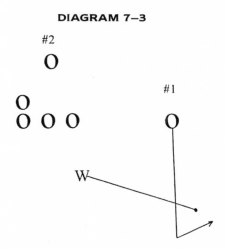

DIAGRAM 7—4

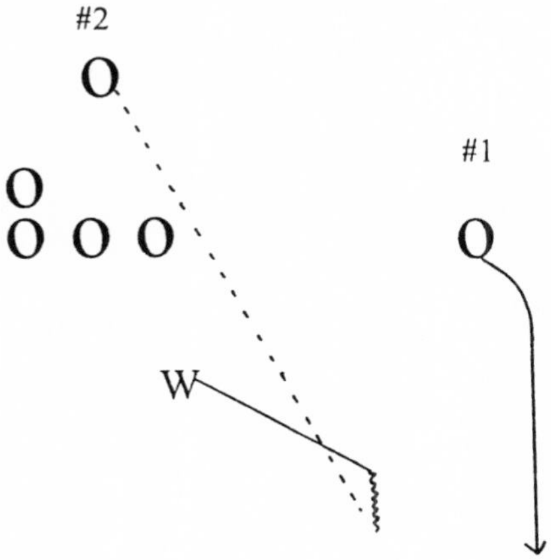

When the offense employs no wide receiver, the outside linebacker recognizes there is no Curl zone. He covers the seam pattern and keeps inside leverage on the receiver. (Diagram 7-5)

When the offense employs a wide receiver and a #2, on or near the line of scrimmage, the outside linebacker recognizes #2 as a possible receiving threat between himself and the Curl zone. When #2 executes a vertical release, the outside linebacker hangs inside the receiver until the receiver gets to a depth of twelve to sixteen yards. The outside linebacker then sprints to the Curl zone. At twelve to sixteen yards, the safety picks up #2, and the linebacker is aware of the coverage of the safety. (Diagram 7-6)

DIAGRAM 7—5

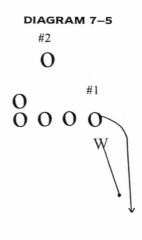

DIAGRAM 7—6

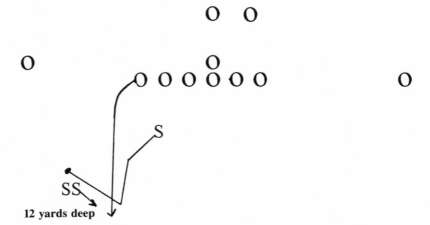

The Mike's responsibility in Blue Spot is the "Hook" zone. The Hook zone is roughly defined as the area between five yards outside of both offensive tackles and twelve to sixteen yards deep. (Diagram 7-7)

This seems like a great deal of area for one defender to cover. However, the Mike does have some help. When #2 executes a vertical release, the outside linebacker hangs inside #2 and then breaks to the Curl zone. This gives the Mike an opportunity to read the eyes of the quarterback and to break in the correct direction.

The Mike also varies his pass drop with the passing action of the quarterback. When the quarterback drops straight back, the Mike covers the Hook zone already defined. (Diagram 7-8)

DIAGRAM 7–7

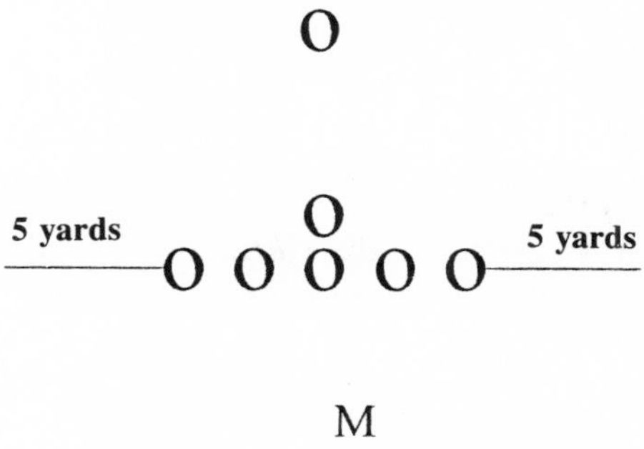

O

5 yards

O

O O O O O

5 yards

M

DIAGRAM 7–8

O   O

O O O O O O   O

M

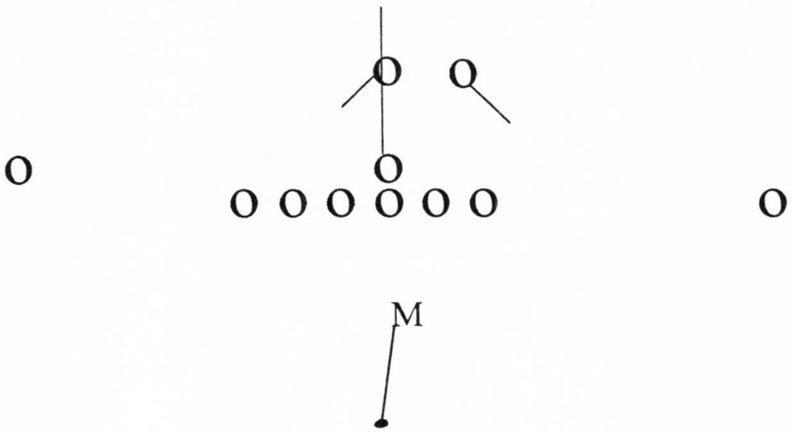

DIAGRAM 7–9

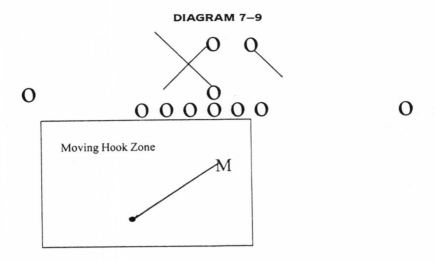

When the quarterback executes a sprint-out or play-action pass, the Hook zone moves with the quarterback and the Mike moves with the zone. The zone does not increase in size. It merely moves with the quarterback. (Diagram 7-9)

Green Spot (Cover 3) (Diagram 7-10)

Green Spot is a three-deep, strong-zone coverage. It may be executed from the Blue Spot alignment or from its own alignment. Blue Spot may also be executed from the Green Spot alignment. This coverage is employed in a definite passing situation.

The corner is a deep one-third zone player. As a general rule, the corner aligns one yard outside of #1, at a depth of eight yards. When the corner reads pass, he drops into the deep one-third zone and covers the deepest receiver in this zone. The corner covers the receiver in his zone by staying deeper than the receiver. The corner takes away the deepest pass and never cuts under the receiver to intercept a ball unless he is SURE of the interception.

The free safety is a deep one-third zone player. The free safety aligns over the guard to the widest receiver side of the formation. The free safety aligns as deep as the widest receiver is from the football. However, he normally does not align deeper than fifteen yards. When the free safety reads pass, he drops into the middle one-third zone and covers the deepest receiver in this zone. Like the corner, the free safety covers the receiver in his zone by staying deeper than the receiver. As the quarterback moves parallel to the line of scrimmage (sprint-out or

DIAGRAM 7—10

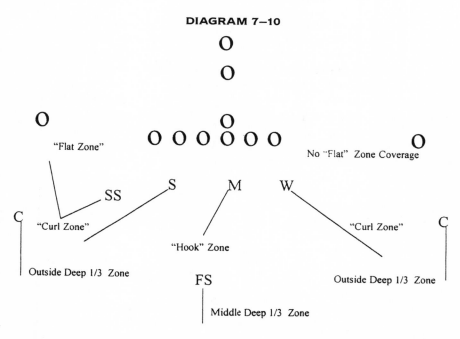

play-action pass), the safety flows with the quarterback. Versus a sprint-out or play-action pass, the free safety is very aware of the backside post pattern and listens for the backside corner's call of "Post." (Diagram 7-11)

DIAGRAM 7—11

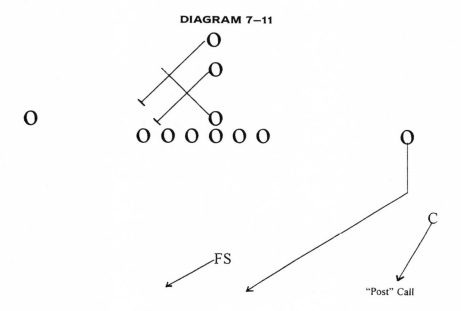

The strong safety is responsible for the strongside Curl-to-Flat zone. He generally aligns three yards outside #2 at a depth of six yards. When the strong safety recognizes a pass play, he sprints toward the wide receiver and the Curl zone. On his way to the Curl zone, the strong safety looks to the flat for any potential receiver. When a receiver shows up in the Flat zone, the strong safety does not fly up to cover him. Instead, he hangs back to undercover the Curl route and give the outside linebacker time to get there. The strong safety is expected to permit a receiver in the Flat zone to catch the ball, unless he is sure of an interception, and then to come up and make a "bone-jarring" hit. (Diagram 7-12)

When the wide receiver executes an out pattern, instead of a Curl pattern, the strong safety is expected to cover the out pattern as part of his Curl to Flat coverage responsibility. (Diagram 7-13)

DIAGRAM 7–12

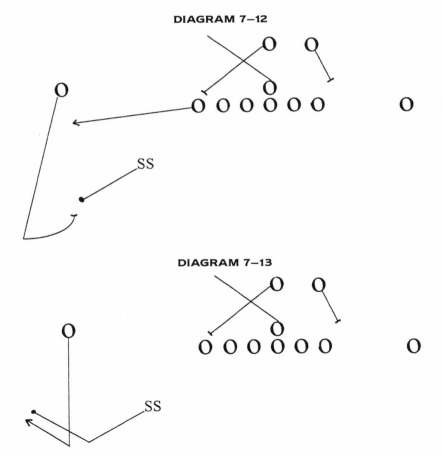

DIAGRAM 7–13

Basically, the linebackers have the same responsibilities in Green Spot as they do in Blue Spot. However, there is one slight change. The Will does not have a Flat zone defender to his side, and this means the Flat zone is not covered. This is a weakness of Green Spot and one reason the coverage is employed in long-yardage situations. If the ball is thrown to a player in the Flat zone, the Will is expected to make the tackle.

Green Spot has several variations. The most commonly used is Green Spot Flat. In this coverage, the strong safety and the Sam exchange pass-coverage responsibilities. On a pass play, the Sam starts toward the Curl zone but is responsible for the Flat zone. The strong safety covers the Curl zone and not the Flat zone. This coverage is used as a change-up and can give the quarterback some key-reading problems. (Diagram 7-14)

DIAGRAM 7–14

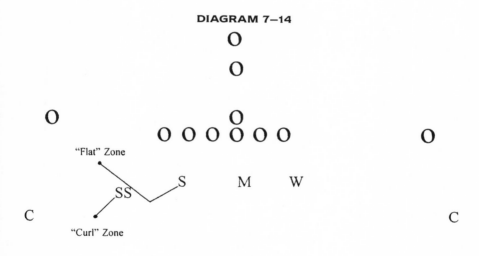

MAN-TO-MAN COVERAGES

There are various techniques used in playing man-to-man coverage. At Widener, inside man-to-man is the rule. The defenders play between the quarterback and the offensive player being covered. This takes away the short completion and forces the quarterback to throw over the defender. Since man-to-man coverages are used with the blitzing game (Chapter 8), forcing the quarterback to throw longer passes gives the blitzers additional time to get the sack or, at least, to hurry the pass.

Red (Pure Man-to-Man Coverage)
(Diagram 7-15)

Red may be executed from three different alignments. It may be executed from the Blue Spot alignment. On the snap of the ball, the defenders move to inside leverage on their receivers. However, from this alignment, the safeties cannot quickly cover #2. There are times when this works in favor of the defense. The quarterback sees the #2 receivers as open and quickly passes the ball to one of them. The safety, flying up to cover #2, puts on a tremendous hit and often separates the receiver from the ball. (Diagram 7-16)

DIAGRAM 7–15

"4 Across the Board" Alignment

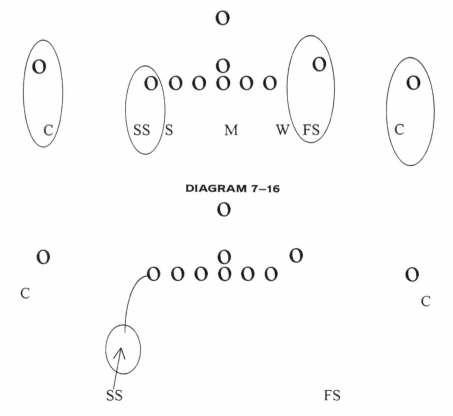

DIAGRAM 7–16

Red may also be executed from the "4-across-the-board" align-ment. (Diagram 7-15) The defensive back aligns on the inside eye of the receiver being covered, at a depth of five yards. There is no disguise with this alignment, and the quarterback reads it as a man-to-man coverage.

The last alignment employed for Red coverage is the "press" alignment. The defensive backs, aligned against split receivers, align on the inside shoulder of the receiver as tight to the line of scrimmage as possible. The defensive backs, not aligned on a wide receiver, employ the 4-across-the-board alignment. (Diagram 7-17) This alignment also gives away man-to-man coverage. However, this alignment is often used as a disguise and, on the snap of the ball, the defensive backs move to some type of zone or combination coverage.

DIAGRAM 7–17

"Press" Alignment

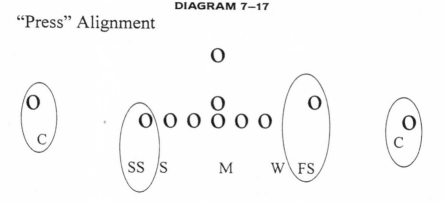

When Red coverage is used, the corners cover the #1's. The safeties cover the #2's and, depending on the blitz being used, the linebackers are responsible for the #3's.

Pink (Soft Man-to-Man Coverage)

Pink may be employed from the Blue Spot alignment or the 4-across-the-board alignment. It may also be executed from the press alignment, but this is rare. Pink is only employed when a seven- or eight-man blitz is being used.

The defensive backs cover the same offensive personnel as in Red coverage. However, when all three linebackers are involved in a blitz, the outside linebacker executes a technique called "Blitz Peel" in covering #3 to his side. This technique is covered in Chapter 8.

When two of the linebackers are involved with the blitz, the linebacker, not blitzing, picks up #3 to one side, and one of the blitzers picks up #3 to the other side. The blitzing linebacker employs the Blitz Peel technique.

Pink coverage is the same as Red coverage except the defensive backs play off the receivers. The goal of the defensive back is to stop the long completion and tackle the short completion. Since this coverage is used in conjunction with an all-out blitz, a sack—or at least a hurry—is expected. The defensive back never attempts to intercept a short pass unless he is absolutely sure he can intercept or knock the ball down. For this reason, the defensive back maintains a four-yard cushion on the receiver until the receiver achieves a depth of twelve to sixteen yards.

COMBINATION COVERAGES

Aspects of both zone coverage and man-to-man coverage are included in a combination coverage. These coverages can all be employed from the Blue Spot alignment, and this eliminates any effective pre-snap read by the quarterback.

Silver

This coverage is always executed from the Blue Spot alignment. The secondary players are employing a form of deep man-to-man coverage, while the linebackers are playing a form of zone coverage. Silver is used in run down situations as the coverage is extremely effective in involving the safeties in defending the running game.

Employing man-to-man coverage, the corner covers #1 or whoever becomes #1 after the snap of the ball. When using either Red coverage or Pink coverage, the corner aligns on the pre-snap alignment of #1 and covers him, no matter what route is run. Silver is somewhat similar to Blue Spot in the fact that the coverage is dependent upon the pattern of #2. When #2 runs a route, other than a route that is to the outside and horizontal, the safety covers him. On the snap of the ball, the corner moves from his outside alignment on #1 to an inside position on #1.

When #2 runs a route that is to the outside and horizontal, the safety to that side makes an "out" call. This call tells the corner to pick up #2 who, by running a route that could take him outside the initial alignment of #1, becomes #1. As in Blue Spot, the corner does not come up and jump the horizontal route but sinks to help undercover the route of the wide receiver, giving the safety additional time to get to his coverage responsibility.

The safety also reads the pattern of #2. When #2 runs a route, other than a route that is to the outside and horizontal, the safety covers #2. However, because of the underneath coverage by the linebackers, the safety does not pick up #2 until he reaches a depth of twelve to sixteen yards.

When #2 runs a route that is to the outside and horizontal, the safety to that side makes an "out" call. The safety then focuses on #1, who becomes #2, and covers him using man-to-man coverage. (Diagram 7-18)

DIAGRAM 7—18

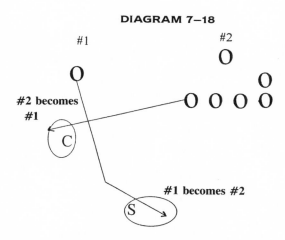

Versus the pass, the secondary play in Silver coverage is very similar to Blue Spot. However, versus the running game, the play of the safeties in Silver is quite different than the play of the safeties in Blue Spot, and this is one reason Silver is used in run down situations. Since the safety is covering #2 with man-to-man coverage, he is using #2 as his key. When #2 blocks for the run, the safety flies to the ball and becomes an additional linebacker. (Diagram 7-19) This allows the defense the luxury of having nine defenders against the running game.

From a secondary standpoint, Silver, like Blue Spot, has a potential weakness. When both #1 and #2 release vertically, the safety is expected to cover #2. Offensive coaches may put the fastest receivers at the #2 positions, and this forces the safeties, not the best cover men in the secondary, to cover the outstanding receivers of the offense. The defensive coach must recognize this possibility and be prepared to adjust to it.

DIAGRAM 7–19

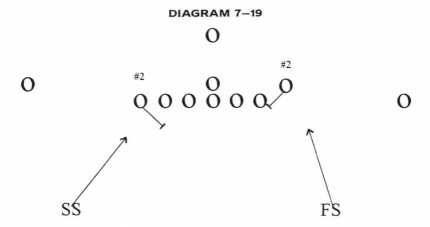

The coverage responsibilities of the linebackers are unique in Silver coverage. The outside linebackers are responsible for the area from outside the offensive tackle to the sideline, to a depth of twelve yards. This seems like a tremendous area to cover. However, both the safety and the corner are playing man-to-man coverage on #1 and #2, and the outside linebacker is responsible to cover any short route run by #2 or any short crossing route by the #2 from the other side of the formation. (Diagram 7-20) The outside linebacker is also responsible for any route by #3 in his area of responsibility.

The Mike is responsible for the area from the offensive tackle to the offensive tackle, to a depth of twelve yards. Like the outside linebacker, he is responsible for any short patterns by #2 and any patterns by #3 in his area of responsibility.

DIAGRAM 7–20

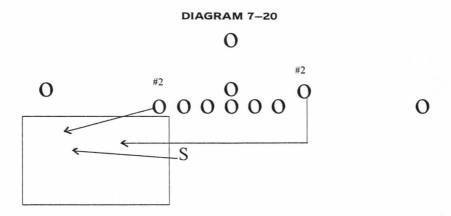

Gold (Diagram 7-21)

Gold coverage is Silver coverage to the strongside and Blue Spot to the weakside. It is Widener's version of the very popular quarter, quarter, half coverage. It is often executed from Blue Spot alignment, but to the weakside, press alignment is also used by the corner.

The corner, strong safety, the Sam, and the Mike execute Silver coverage. The corner, free safety, and the Will employ Blue Spot coverage.

This is an excellent coverage to employ against the running game or passing game. The strongside of the defense has all the benefits of Silver coverage versus the running game, while the weakside of the defense can easily discourage the quick passing game by the use of the rolled-up corner.

DIAGRAM 7—21

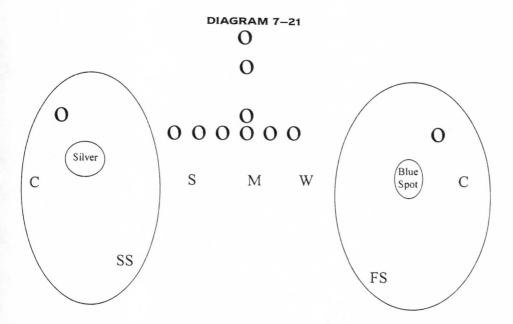

Green (Diagram 7-22)

Green is similar to Green Spot with several exceptions. Green may be executed from the Blue Spot alignment or from a Green Spot alignment. It is most often employed from the Green Spot alignment with the intent of giving the quarterback a false pre-snap read. It is

DIAGRAM 7—22

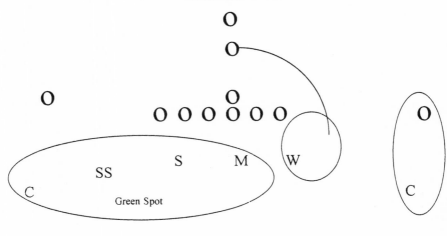

DIAGRAM 7—23

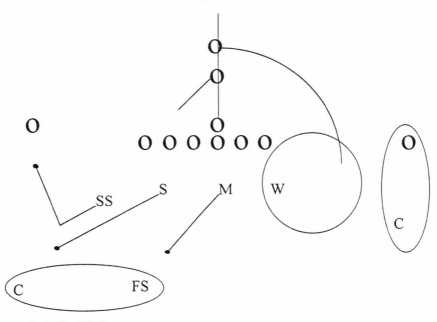

Looks like 1/4's Coverage

hoped the quarterback will read the alignment as Green Spot (a strong zone coverage) and think the weakside Flat zone is open. However, this is not the case.

For the strongside corner, strong safety, the Sam, and the Mike, Green coverage is basically the same as Green Spot. For the free safety, the Will, and the weakside corner Green coverage is totally different.

On the snap of the ball, the free safety moves to an alignment two yards outside the original alignment of the strongside offensive tackle, while maintaining his normal Green Spot Depth. From this position, the free safety becomes a strongside middle one-third player. Instead of playing in the middle of the deep one-third zone, as he does in Green Spot, the free safety moves to the strongside of that zone. With the strongside corner in the deep outside one-third zone and the free safety in the strongside of the middle one-third zone, it looks very much like a form of quarters coverage. (Diagram 7-23)

The weakside corner covers the weakside #1 with man-to-man coverage, and the Will covers the weakside #2 with man-to-man coverage. Will's coverage is not difficult when #2 is a running back coming out for a pass. However, when #2 is a wide receiver in a slot alignment, this coverage is checked to another coverage or a "Match" call puts the secondary into a different coverage to keep the Will from having to cover a speedy wide receiver.

Green coverage provides excellent strongside deep pass coverage by allowing the free safety to disregard the post pattern from a weakside receiver, since the weakside #1 is covered by the weakside corner. Man-to-man coverage on the weakside of the formation takes away the open weakside Flat zone, not covered in Green Spot. This coverage is employed against an offense that has a tendency to attack the strongside with its passing game.

Orange (Man-Free Coverage) (Diagram 7-24)

Orange coverage is normally employed with a blitz. It is man-to-man coverage with a free safety playing the deep middle zone. It may be executed from Blue Spot, Green Spot, or 4-across-the-board alignment.

Both corners cover the #1 to their side. The strong safety covers the #2 to the strong side. The free safety plays as though it is Green Spot coverage. The linebackers are responsible for the #2 to the weakside and the #3 to either side. The linebacker coverage is determined by the blitz being used. The coverage is a Blitz Peel when a blitzing linebacker has to cover a receiver.

DIAGRAM 7—24

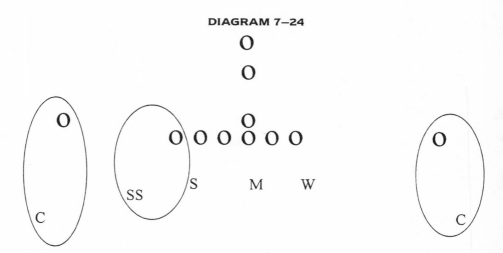

The coverages described in this chapter are those most commonly used by teams who employ the 4-3 Defense. However, there are many other coverages used by various 4-3 defensive teams. There are also many 4-3 defensive teams who employ only three or four different coverages. The number of coverages used is strictly a decision of the defensive coach.

8

The 4-3 Blitz Package

Most 4-3 defensive teams employ similar blitz packages. The main differences occur in the various methods employed for calling a blitz. This chapter covers the basic 4-3 blitz package with some of the Widener methods of calling these blitzes.

SHOW AND TRICK

Show and Trick were discussed in Chapter 1. However, the importance of these two facets of the defense cannot be over-emphasized. They keep the offensive team off balance and help make the blitzing game much more effective. The use of these two elements of the defense eliminates the effectiveness of a quarterback calling an audible versus what he perceives to be a blitzing defense.

The three-, four-, seven- and eight-man blitzes (known as "Numbered Blitzes") can be run from the Show alignment or a normal linebacker depth alignment. Key Blitz must be run from a front with the linebackers aligned at a normal depth.

NUMBERED BLITZES

These blitzes are named by identifying the number of players involved with the blitz. A Three Blitz involves two defensive linemen and one linebacker. Therefore, the blitz is called a Three Blitz. All numbered blitzes are primarily used in passing situations for the purpose of getting a sack or, at least, hurrying the pass.

Three Blitz

The Three Blitz involves the weakside defensive tackle, the weakside defensive end, and the Will—or the strongside defensive tackle, the strongside defensive end, and the Sam. Mike is not involved with the Three Blitz. The blitz may be called to the weakside, strongside or on a rare occasion, to both sides. When Show is used, the blitzing linebacker uses his Show alignment. The other two linebackers (not blitzing) may use the Trick alignment or their normal alignment. The blitz may also be executed with all three linebackers in the normal alignment.

Since the Three Blitz requires a defensive end in a 5 alignment and an outside linebacker in a 50 alignment, the Three Blitz is normally executed to the weakside only. However, when the strongside of the offensive formation has no tight end or tight slot, the Three Blitz can be executed to the strongside.

When the Three Blitz is employed to the weakside, the defensive tackle and end execute their pass rush in their normal pass-rush lanes. The Will blitzes through the "B" gap. (Diagram 8-1)

DIAGRAM 8—1

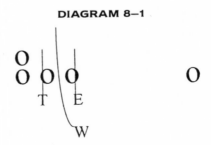

When the Three Blitz is executed to the strongside, the defensive tackle, in a 3 alignment, must rush across the face of the guard and pass rush through the A gap. The defensive tackle may slightly adjust his 3 alignment, before the snap of the ball, to put himself closer to the A gap. The defensive end executes his normal pass rush, and the Sam blitzes through the strongside B gap. (Diagram 8-2) Since there is no blitz allowing two players to go through one gap, it is impractical to use Show for this blitz. Show would initially put both the Sam and the strongside defensive tackle in the B gap. (Diagram 8-3)

DIAGRAM 8–2

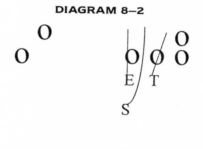

DIAGRAM 8–3

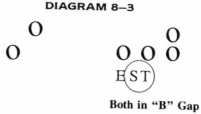

Both in "B" Gap

DIAGRAM 8–4

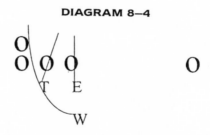

The Three Blitz can also be used with a crossing action between the defensive tackle and the blitzing linebacker. When this is used, the letter "X" follows the blitz call in the huddle. This blitz is most effective versus a drop-back passing game.

When Three Blitz Weak X is used, the weakside defensive end executes his normal pass rush. The weakside defensive tackle, in a 2i alignment, rushes across the face of the guard and attacks B gap. The defensive tackle may slightly adjust his 2i alignment, prior to the snap of the ball, to put himself closer to the B gap. The Will, from his 50 alignment, blitzes through the A gap. (Diagram 8-4) For the same reasons as the Three Blitz Strong, the Show alignment is not used with this blitz.

The Three Blitz X can also be employed to the strongside. The defensive tackle and end execute their normal pass rush, and the Sam blitzes through the strongside A gap. (Diagram 8-5)

DIAGRAM 8—5

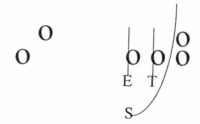

Four Blitz

This blitz involves the same defensive personnel as the Three Blitz, with the addition of the Mike. The blitz may be called to the weakside or the strongside but, since it involves the Mike, it can never be employed to both sides. When Show is used, the Mike and the blitzing outside linebacker may use the Show alignment. The other outside linebacker may use the Trick alignment or his normal alignment. The Four Blitz may also be executed with all three linebackers in their normal alignment.

Unlike the Three Blitz, the Four Blitz can be used versus a tight end or tight slot. When the blitz is executed to the strongside, versus a tight end or tight slot, the defensive tackle and end perform their normal pass rush. The Sam blitzes the strongside C gap, and the Mike blitzes the strongside A gap. (Diagram 8-6)

DIAGRAM 8—6

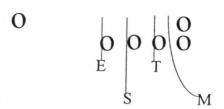

When the blitz is employed to the strongside versus a formation with no tight end or tight slot, there is no change for the defensive tackle or the Mike. However, there are changes for the defensive end and the Sam. The Sam still blitzes the C gap but goes outside the defensive end. The defensive end executes a charge similar to the Texas charge (Chapter 6). The defensive end begins his normal pass rush, but aims his charge at the outside ear of the offensive tackle. The end maintains contact with the offensive tackle until the Sam goes by him. The defensive end steps outside and parallel to the line of scrimmage and then rushes the passer. The defensive end becomes the outside pass rusher and the outside contain man. (Diagram 8-7) The Show alignment can be employed by the Sam in this situation, and it presents an interesting look to the offensive team. (Diagram 8-8)

DIAGRAM 8—7

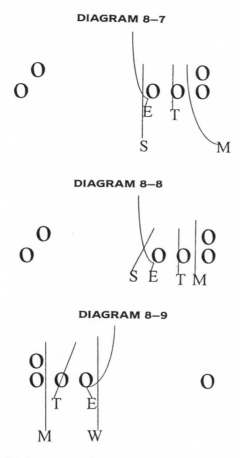

DIAGRAM 8—8

DIAGRAM 8—9

When the blitz is executed to the weakside versus no tight end or tight slot, the weakside defensive end and the Will employ the same techniques used by the Sam and the strongside defensive end in the strongside blitz. The weakside tackle employs the same techniques used with the Three Blitz Weak X, and the Mike blitzes the weakside A gap. (Diagram 8-9) The Show alignment cannot be used by the Mike.

When the blitz is used to the weakside versus a tight end, there is no change for the defensive tackle and the Mike. The weakside defensive end, in a 5 alignment, executes his normal pass rush. The Will, in a 7 alignment, blitzes the D gap. (Diagram 8-10)

Like the Three Blitz, the Four Blitz can also be used with a crossing action between the defensive tackle and the Mike. When this is used, X follows the blitz call in the huddle. The X call has no effect on the outside linebacker or the defensive end.

When Four Blitz Strong X is employed, the defensive tackle, in a 3 alignment, goes across the face of the guard and rushes through the strongside A gap. The Mike blitzes through the strongside B Gap. (Diagram 8-11) The Show alignment cannot be used by the Mike with this blitz.

When Four Blitz Weak X is used, the defensive tackle, in a 2i alignment, employs his normal pass rush. The Mike blitzes the weakside B gap. (Diagram 8-12)

DIAGRAM 8–10

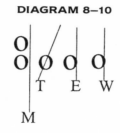

DIAGRAM 8–11

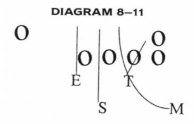

DIAGRAM 8–12

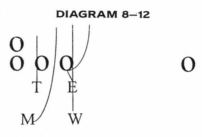

Seven and Eight Blitz (All-Out Blitzes)

With so many modern offensive teams using the quick passing game with four receivers on or near the line of scrimmage, it is becoming more and more difficult to get to the passer with a Three or Four Blitz package. The seven- and eight-man blitz packages, with some form of man-to-man pass coverage, have become very popular. The Seven and Eight Blitzes complement the blitzes already discussed in this chapter.

Use of either the Seven or Eight Blitz is determined by the number of receivers on or near the line of scrimmage. The blitz is called in the huddle as "Seven Blitz." However, when the offense snaps the ball with two running backs in the backfield, the blitz can automatically become an Eight Blitz. The free safety becomes an additional blitzer to the single-receiver side of the offense. The three receivers, on or near the line of scrimmage, are covered by the two corners and the strong safety. (Diagram 8-13)

DIAGRAM 8—13

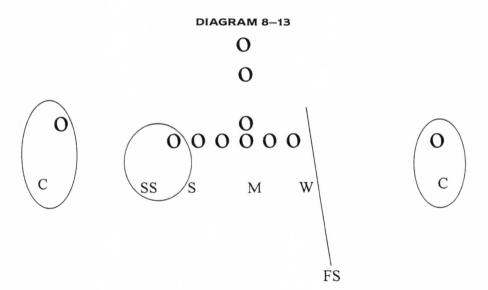

When the offense employs a single-back set, the four receivers are covered by the four defensive backs, and no member of the secondary can execute a blitz. (Diagram 8-14)

When the Seven Blitz is used, the front defenders rush through gaps they are responsible for versus the run, and the Mike normally blitzes through the strongside A gap. Versus an offensive set with seven gaps, this blitz leaves no gap uncovered. (Diagram 8-15) This blitz can be executed from a Show alignment and this is the basic look when Trick is employed, and there is no blitz called. (Diagram 8-16) When this blitz is executed against this set with two backs in the backfield (becomes an Eight Blitz), the free safety becomes the extra blitzer. He blitzes from the outside and becomes a weakside D gap defender. (Diagram 8-17)

DIAGRAM 8—14

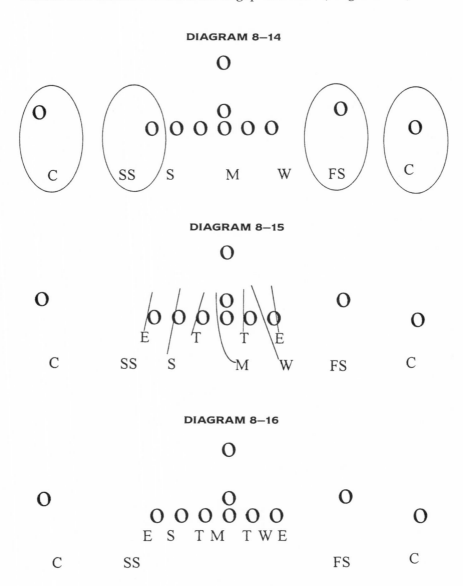

DIAGRAM 8—15

DIAGRAM 8—16

DIAGRAM 8–17

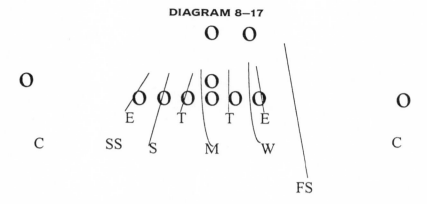

When the Seven Blitz is employed versus an offensive set with eight gaps, the weakside B gap is not defended. The weakside tackle and end are made aware of this weakness and must alter their rush lanes to compensate for this weakness. However, when there are two backs in the backfield (becomes an Eight Blitz), the free safety blitzes through the weakside B gap and there is no undefended gap. (Diagram 8-18)

DIAGRAM 8–18

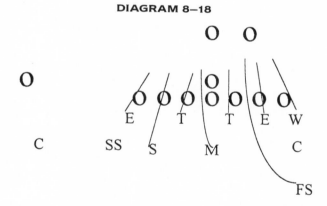

When "X" is called with the Seven Blitz, the Mike and the strongside tackle employ the same techniques as a Four Blitz Strong X. (Diagram 8-19) When this is called, the Mike cannot employ a Show alignment.

When a Seven Blitz is used against an offensive set with one back in the backfield, this back must be covered if he releases for a pass. This is accomplished by employing the Blitz Peel. All three linebackers blitz toward the single back. When the back steps toward one of the

DIAGRAM 8—19

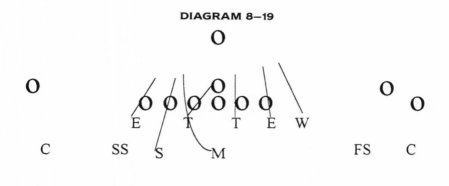

DIAGRAM 8—20

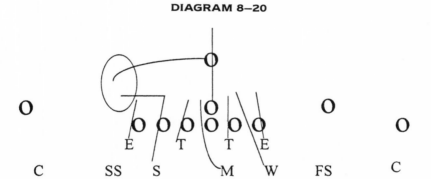

linebackers or releases in the direction of the linebacker, that linebacker picks the back up and covers him using man-to-man techniques. The linebacker is also allowed to knock the back down. However, the linebacker cannot miss the back and allow him to be free to catch a pass. The other two linebackers continue the blitz and rush the quarterback. (Diagram 8-20)

When a "Seven Blitz" is used against an offensive set with seven gaps and two backs in the backfield (becomes an Eight Blitz), either back must be covered if he releases for a pass. The Will has no Blitz Peel responsibility since the free safety blitzes outside of him. The free safety picks up the Blitz Peel responsibility. (Diagram 8-21)

When a Seven Blitz is used against an offensive set with eight gaps and two backs in the backfield (becomes an Eight Blitz), the Will maintains his Blitz Peel responsibility. The free safety does not have Blitz Peel responsibility since he is blitzing the weakside B gap. (Diagram 8-22)

DIAGRAM 8—21

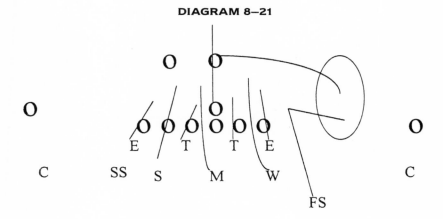

DIAGRAM 8—22

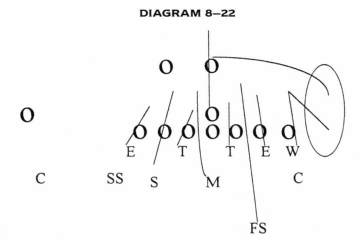

KEY BLITZ

This blitz is used in running situations. The main purpose of the blitz is to confuse offensive blocking patterns. By using this blitz, the defense immediately fills all the gaps to the side of the running play. It is most effective when all three linebackers are aligned off the line of scrimmage. However, it may still be used when an outside linebacker is employing a 7 alignment.

DIAGRAM 8–23

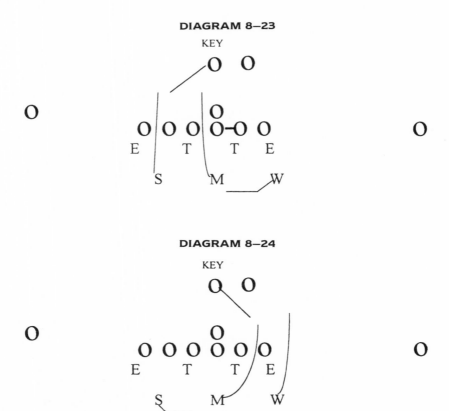

The four down linemen execute their normal techniques. The linebackers key one back. This back is determined by the scouting report. The direction of the blitz is determined by the direction of the key. When the key goes to the strongside of the formation, the Sam immediately blitzes the strongside C gap, and the Mike blitzes the strongside A gap. All strongside gaps are now filled with defenders. The Will executes his normal hitman technique. (Diagram 8-23)

When the key goes to the weakside of the formation, the Will immediately blitzes the D gap, and the Mike blitzes the weakside B gap. All weakside gaps are now filled with defenders. The Sam executes his normal hitman technique. (Diagram 8-24)

In this chapter many of the basic 4-3 blitzes have been covered. The number of possible blitzes is limited only by the imagination of the defensive coach.

9

The 4-3 Nickel Package

The passing game has become the main weapon of many teams. The popularity of the passing game has grown with the use of two, three, or four wide receivers and running backs who can effectively catch the ball. Since many offensive teams, in passing situations, replace tight ends and running backs with wide receivers, the defense must also adjust by replacing slower personnel with an additional defensive back or two. The defense has to perform this task without severely limiting its ability to stop the run, especially the draw play.

The 4-3 Defense easily adjusts to Nickel situations. At Widener, the Mike is replaced by a defensive back, and the defensive front makes a few minor adjustments, while the secondary uses the basic coverages with one major variation.

FRONTS

The main defensive line adjustment, in a passing situation, is to replace the defensive ends with quicker personnel. Having quicker defensive ends is certainly an advantage and perhaps too much of a luxury for many teams. For those teams that do not get enough of a pass rush with their four down linemen, a blitz package is a requirement, and an excellent blitz package is described later in this chapter. Various line stunts including Texas, Tom It and Ed It (Chapter 6) are also employed to facilitate a better pass rush.

For the defensive linemen, the Nickel Package begins with a basic 4-3 alignment. (Diagram 9-1) The defensive linemen have their normal gap responsibilities with a little less concern about the running game. Normally, one of the defensive tackles is given the responsibility to defend against the middle screen and draw plays.

The linebacker adjustments are a bit more complicated. A fifth defensive back (the reason it is called Nickel) replaces a linebacker, normally the Mike. Depending on the secondary coverage employed, the fifth defensive back (Nickel back) may play a linebacker position or a defensive back position.

The outside linebackers adjust their alignments and run down responsibilities. Versus most offensive sets, and with most secondary calls, the Sam stacks behind the strongside tackle (30 alignment). When the offense employs a tight end or tight slot versus the running game, the Sam is responsible for the strongside A and C gaps. (Diagram 9-2) When there is no tight end or tight slot versus the running game, the Sam is responsible for the strongside A gap. (Diagram 9-3) The Sam's pass responsibilities depend on the coverage being employed.

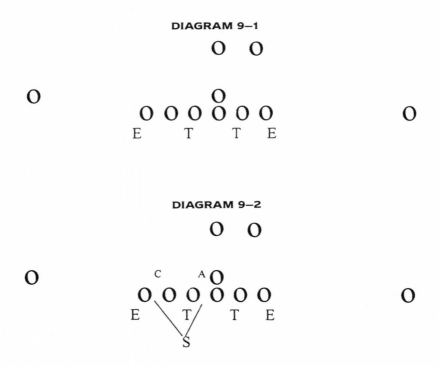

DIAGRAM 9–1

DIAGRAM 9–2

DIAGRAM 9–3

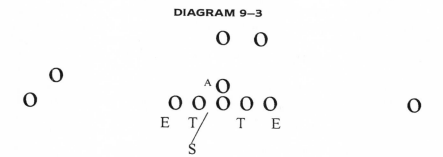

Versus most offensive sets, and with most secondary calls, the Will also makes use of a 30 alignment. The Will is responsible for the weakside B gap versus a running play. (Diagram 9-4) When the offense makes use of a tight end or tight slot to the weakside, the Will does not change his alignment or gap responsibility. All adjustments are made by the defensive backs. This simplifies the responsibilities of the two linebackers.

DIAGRAM 9–4

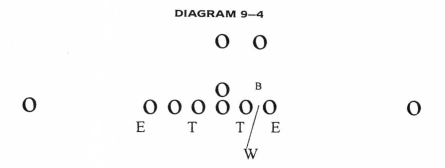

SECONDARIES

The coverages in Nickel Situations are called in the same manner as in normal situations. One coverage may be called and used against all formations. Two coverages may be called in the huddle and used according to the offensive formation or a "Match" call may be used. As in normal situations, coverage disguises are employed to confuse pre-snap reads.

In Nickel Situations, many of the basic coverages are employed. The most commonly used coverages are Blue Spot, Green Spot, Orange (used with certain linebacker blitzes), Black (five-under, two-deep, man-to-man coverage) and a unique coverage called "Hot."

There are two distinct philosophies when it comes to secondary play in the Nickel Situation. The first is to rush four defensive linemen and play coverage with the other seven defenders. Widener does this with the Blue Spot, Green Spot, and Black coverages.

The second philosophy involves sending more than four pass rushers (using a blitz) while employing some type of man-to-man coverage. Widener does this with the Orange and Hot coverages.

When Blue Spot is used, the Nickel back assumes the linebacker position and pass responsibilities. The Nickel back aligns to the strong-side of the formation but varies his alignment according to the placement of the strongside #2 receiver. The pass responsibilities of the Nickel back are the same as the Sam in a normal situation. The Nickel back is responsible for the Curl. The Sam plays as the Mike does in a normal situation, and the Will plays his normal Hook responsibility. (Diagram 9-5)

When Green Spot is used in Nickel Situation, the Nickel back becomes an additional strong safety and plays to the weakside of the

DIAGRAM 9–5

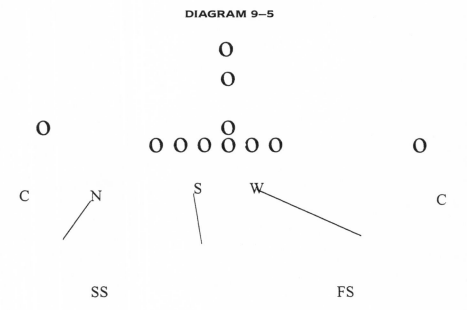

formation. The Nickel back employs the same alignments and responsibilities as the strong safety in normal situations, except to the
weakside. The two outside linebackers use the same techniques that
they employ in a normal situation. The short middle zone is left
undefended, and this is a weakness in the coverage. However, in a long-
yardage situation, it is worth the gamble. The linebackers slightly
modify their pass drops to compensate for this weakness. (Diagram 9-6)

DIAGRAM 9–6

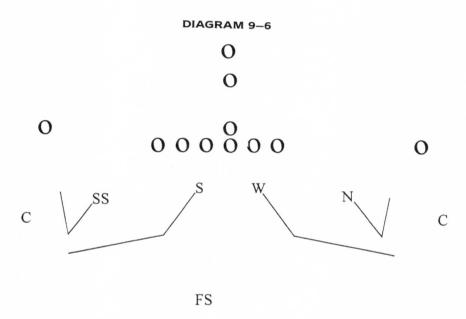

When Black is employed, the Nickel back becomes a man-to-man
player and covers the strongside #2. The Will is responsible for the
weakside #2 and the Sam is responsible for #3 to either side. Depending on the offensive formation employed, the linebackers may have to
alter their basic Nickel alignments. Versus any offensive set with two
backs in the backfield, the linebackers use the Nickel alignment.

When the offense employs a one-back set, adjustments are necessary. When the offense is in a balanced formation, two receivers to each
side, the Will moves out to cover the weakside #2. As in all man-to-man
coverages, the Will plays the receiver on the inside. The Sam moves to
the Mike position and, versus the run, is responsible for the strongside
A and weakside B gaps. (Diagram 9-7)

DIAGRAM 9—7

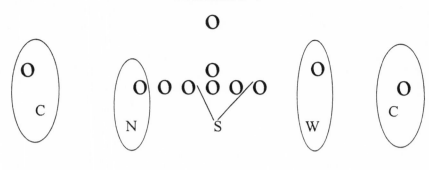

SS   FS

When the offense makes use of a Trips formation, the Sam moves out and covers the strongside #3, and the Will moves to the Mike position. Depending on personnel, the Sam may stay at the Mike position, and the Will may move over to cover the strongside #3. (Diagram 9-8)

DIAGRAM 9—8

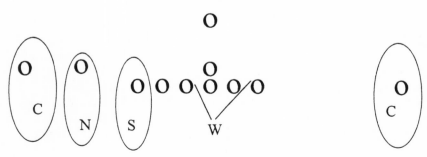

SS   FS

The safeties use the same techniques employed with Blue Spot coverage. They are half-field defenders. The corners use the same techniques as Red coverage. Normally, the corner employs a Lock alignment on the inside of the receiver.

When Orange is used as the secondary coverage, the front is involved with a blitz. In the Nickel Situation, Orange is always employed from a Green Spot alignment. The Nickel back is responsible for man-to-man coverage on the weakside #2. The linebackers are responsible for #3. When the linebacker is blitzing and #3 comes to his side, the linebacker employs his Blitz Peel technique and covers #3. (Diagram 9-9)

DIAGRAM 9—9

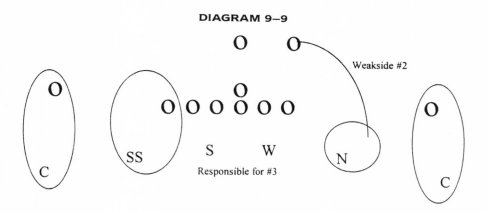

FS

When the offense makes use of a Trips set, either the strong safety or the Nickel back covers #3. The linebacker away from the Trips is responsible for the weakside #2, and the other linebacker is responsible for strongside #4 and weakside #3.

In the Nickel Situation, Trick and Show are used, and a blitz may be run from a normal or Show alignment. The most commonly used blitzes are the Three Blitzes and, on occasion, a Three Blitz is employed to both sides of the formation. A blitz to both sides can occur only when there is no tight end or tight slot to either side. (Diagram 9-10) When the Three Blitz is called to both sides and the offense comes out with a tight end to either side, the blitz is checked off to that side.

DIAGRAM 9–10

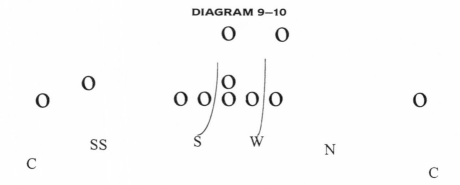

FS

HOT VARIATION

The "Hot" variation is a unique approach to a Nickel Situation. It is an extremely aggressive method of handling long-yardage situations. The front six defenders use the same alignments as in the basic Nickel alignments. The secondary initially aligns in the Green Spot alignment. From this point, an unusual and very effective defense evolves.

The secondary defenders and the linebackers are assigned numbers starting with the defensive left as follows:

- Left Corner—#1
- Strong Safety—#2
- Sam—#3
- Free Safety—#4
- Will—#5
- Nickel Back—#6
- Right Corner—#7 (Diagram 9-11)

Hot always involves two blitzers, and these are designated by the numbers called in the huddle. As an example, when "23" is called in the huddle, the strong safety and the Sam are involved with the blitz. There are several blitz rules observed in the Hot defense:

1. All blitzes from the corner come from the outside. Versus a formation with a tight end, the blitz comes from outside the tight end (D gap). (Diagram 9-12) Versus a formation with a split end, the blitz comes outside the defensive end (D gap). The corner must "Cheat Up" prior to the blitz. (Diagram 9-13)

DIAGRAM 9—11

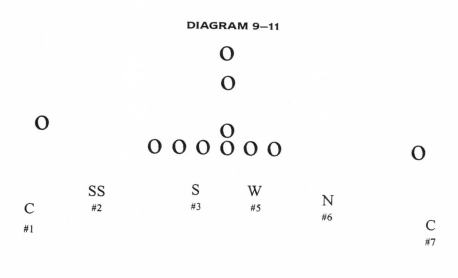

DIAGRAM 9—12

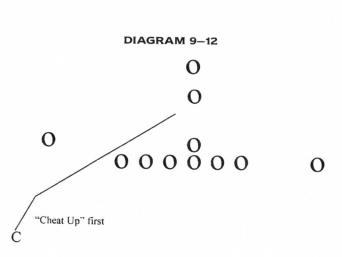

DIAGRAM 9–13

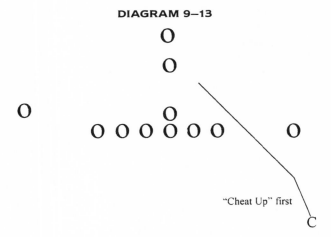

"Cheat Up" first

2. The strongside corner, strong safety, and the Sam can only blitz the strongside of the formation. The weakside corner, free safety, Nickel back, and the Will can only blitz the weakside of the formation.

3. All blitzes, other than corner blitzes, are in the strongside A gap, the weakside B gap, or either D gap. This is determined by the call. For example, when the call in the huddle is "Nickel – 25 – Hot," the Will blitzes the weakside B gap. Since the strongside A gap is not being blitzed by a linebacker, the strong safety blitzes that gap. (Diagram 9-14) When the huddle call is "Nickel – 23 – Hot," the Sam blitzes the strongside A gap. Since the strongside A gap is taken, the strong safety blitzes the strong-side D gap. (Diagram 9-15)

4. The free safety has the power to change the blitz, when he sees the offensive formation being employed. When "Nickel – 26 – Hot" is called and the offense comes out in a four-receiver, double-slot formation, the free safety has to change the blitz call. If the strong safety and the Nickel back were allowed to blitz, the two slots would be immediately open for a quick pass reception. Seeing this possibility, the free safety checks to "35." This call makes the two linebackers the blitzers and allows the strong safety and Nickel back to play coverage. (Diagram 9-16)

DIAGRAM 9–14

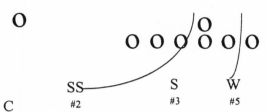

O

O

O   O

O O O O O O

O   O

SS   S   W

                    N

#2   #3   #5

C   #6

#1   C

                          #7

FS

#4

DIAGRAM 9–15

O

O

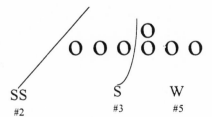

O

O O O O O O

O   O

SS   S   W

                    N

#2   #3   #5

C   #6

#1   C

                          #7

FS

#4

DIAGRAM 9—16

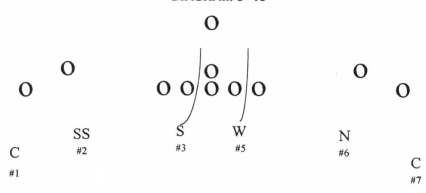

When "Nickel – 15 – Hot" is called in the huddle and the offensive formation being employed has a receiver flanked fifteen yards from the tight end, the free safety has to check the call. The corner cannot be an effective blitzer from such a wide alignment and if he cheats in, prior to the snap, the quarterback could pick it up and hit the flanker with a quick pass. Seeing this problem, the free safety checks to "25." This keeps the corner outside and allows the strong safety to replace him as the blitzer. (Diagram 9-17)

There are times when "Nickel – 0 – Hot" is called in the huddle. This call tells the potential blitzers to listen for the call of the free safety after the offense aligns on the ball. The free safety looks at the formation and makes his blitz call according to the game plan for that particular formation.

Once the blitz is called, two defenders remain as underneath pass defenders, and three defensive backs drop into a three-deep zone secondary. These players are determined by the blitz call. By looking at the previous two huddle calls, and with the understanding that a linebacker is never expected to become a defensive back, this concept becomes clear. When "Nickel – 25 – Hot" is called, both corners and the free safety are not involved with the blitz. They become the three-deep zone defenders, and the Will and Nickel back are the underneath pass defenders. (Diagram 9-18) When "Nickel – 23 – Hot" is called, the three

DIAGRAM 9–17

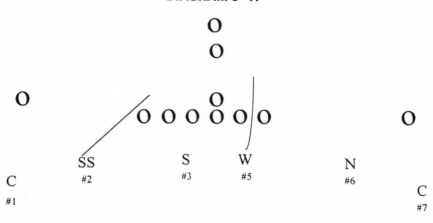

DIAGRAM 9–18

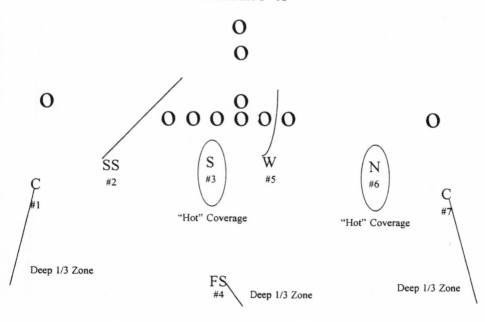

deep defenders remain the same. The two underneath defenders change. (Diagram 9-19)

Normally, the blitz is set up to have one weakside and one strongside blitzer. By doing this, there is an underneath pass defender to the strongside and weakside of the formation. On the snap of the ball, this makes the coverage responsibilities of the underneath defenders a bit simpler.

The underneath pass defender covers (man to man) the first receiver to show to his side of the formation, or what is referred to as the Hot receiver. The underneath pass defender knows there is coverage in the deep zones and the quarterback should be sacked or, at least, forced to throw quickly. This allows the underneath defender to play very aggressively.

When "Nickel – 36 – Hot" is called and the offense comes out in a Pro formation, the Sam and Nickel back execute the blitz. The Sam blitzes the strongside A gap, and the Nickel back blitzes the weakside D gap. This leaves the strong safety and the Will as the underneath Hot defenders. The Will looks for a back out of the backfield, while the strong safety jumps the tight end. (Diagram 9-20)

DIAGRAM 9—19

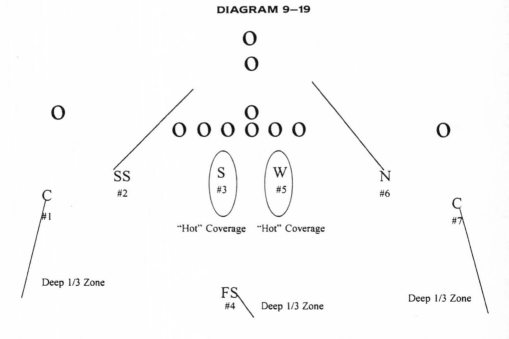

DIAGRAM 9—20

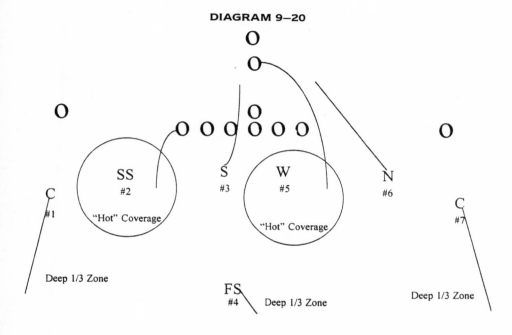

DIAGRAM 9—21

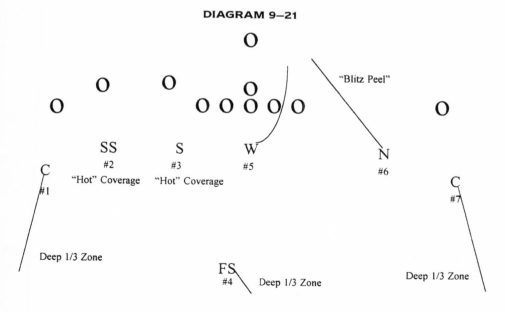

Versus a Trips set, the free safety checks to allow two defenders to blitz from one side of the formation. Versus an offensive formation with Trips to the defensive left and a split end to the defensive right, the free safety checks to "56." This call allows the Will and Nickel back to become the blitzers. The Nickel back knows there is no Hot defender to his side, and he makes use of Blitz Peel if the single back attempts to slip out to his side. The two Hot defenders are the strong safety and the Sam, and they cover #2 and #3 to the strongside. (Diagram 9-21)

The Hot defense does have weaknesses. If the offense sends two Hot receivers to one side of the formation (other than a Trips set), the second receiver could end up uncovered. Formation changes, with motion and pre-snap shifts, cause check calls by the free safety, and the free safety has to be skilled enough to make the checks. These are two of the most significant weaknesses.

When the Hot Defense is used in conjunction with the other Nickel defenses, it is extremely effective. The fact that Green Spot, Orange and Hot are executed from the Green Spot alignment, makes all three more effective because the quarterback gets the same pre-snap read for all three coverages.

Part III

The 4-3 Defense in Action

In Part III, the knowledge acquired in the first two parts of this text is put into action against various offensive plays. The most popular offensive plays and formations are employed for this purpose. The Basic Defense with Cover 2 is shown against each play, and a variation is also shown against each play. A description of each defensive player's reaction to the play is also covered.

Prior to playing against any of the offenses described in this chapter, the defensive team spends a week practicing against each play. This gives the defensive team a familiarity with the expected offense and an idea of what to expect on game day.

10

The 4-3 Vs. the Wing-T Sweep and Trap

One of the most difficult offenses to defend against is the Delaware Wing-T. This was the topic of my second book, *Defensing the Delaware Wing-T.* In that book, the defense described was the 5-2 or 3-4 Defense rather than the 4-3 Defense. However, the 4-3 Defense can also be effective versus this dynamic offensive system.

Two of the most important plays in the Wing-T offense are the Sweep and the Trap. In order to stop, or at least slow down, the Wing-T running game, the Sweep and Trap must be successfully defended. In this chapter, the Sweep and the Trap are described from the basic Wing-T formation (100 formation in the Wing-T terminology) and to the defensive left.

DEFENDING THE SWEEP—
WITH THE
BASIC 4-3 WITH COVER 2

The left (strongside) defensive tackle reads the pull of the right guard. This read is similar to a fold block by the guard and tackle. The defensive tackle steps to the offensive tackle, who is attempting a down block on him. The defensive tackle attempts to push the offensive tackle into the C gap. When he sees the opposite guard attempting a pull to the onside, the defensive tackle can attack that guard and attempt to knock him off his path. This rarely happens due to the depth of the left guard's pull. However, when it does happen, it really helps stop the play. (Diagram 10-1)

DIAGRAM 10–1

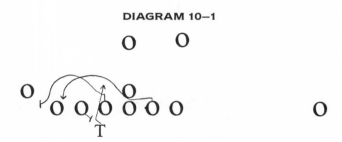

The left (strongside) defensive end reads the down block of the tight end. The defensive end gets his hands on the tight end to flatten the tight end's path to the Sam. This is critical to keeping the tight end off the Sam. As the defensive end turns slightly inside to look for the pulling guard with the hope of wrong arming his block, he is blocked by the wing. As the defensive end feels the pressure of the wing's block, the defensive end fights the pressure and attempts to push the wing to the outside. Even though the wing has a perfect blocking angle on the defensive end, the end is normally much bigger and stronger than the wing and should, at least, get a stalemate at the point of attack.

Versus the Wing-T, the Sam reads the far-set halfback as his initial key. When the Sam sees his key coming toward him and the left guard cross the spot, he assumes the play is Sweep. The Sam looks to the tight end, who he knows is going to attempt to block him. Since the defensive end got his hands on the tight end, the tight end has a poor angle on the Sam, and the Sam flows slightly to the outside, expecting the left guard to attempt to pin him inside. The Sam is one of the defensive players who should make the first hit on this play.

The left corner, versus a wing, aligns five yards deep (rather than his normal six yards deep) and one yard outside the wing (#1). When the corner recognizes the down block by the wing and knows it is not a passing play, the corner comes up and replaces the wing. In other words, the corner ends up on the line of scrimmage directly across from the wing's initial alignment. The corner does NOT cross the line of scrimmage. If the corner came up wider and crossed the line of scrimmage, he would give the lead guard (right guard) a perfect angle to kick the corner out. (Diagram 10-2) By staying on the line of scrimmage and directly across from the wing's initial alignment, the corner gives the lead guard a very difficult, if not impossible, kick-out block. This may force the lead guard to attempt to log block the corner, rather than kick the corner out. The Wing-T guard would much rather execute a kick-out block than a log block, and this can cause problems

DIAGRAM 10–2

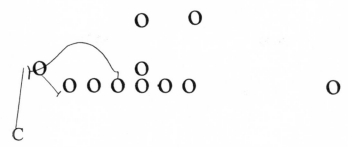

for the lead guard. Like the Sam, the left corner is expected to be one of the first hitters on the play.

The strong safety is slow reacting to the run. Once he recognizes run, he comes up and should make the tackle if the back gets through the front. However, the running back would have, at least, a five-yard gain if the strong safety had to make the play.

The Mike reads the fullback to the set halfback as his initial keys. The Mike sees the fullback step to the defensive right and sees the halfback flow to the defensive left. The Mike also sees the left guard cross the spot. Once the Mike sees the guard cross the spot, he knows the play is either the Trap or the Sweep. The Mike steps up and to the left in an attempt to cover the strongside A gap, in case it is the Trap play and to avoid the attempted block by the center if it is the Sweep. Once the Mike is sure it is not the Trap, he flows to the outside and may get to the ballcarrier before the ballcarrier crosses the line of scrimmage. Often, the tight end cannot block the Sam, and he continues on the same level to pick up the Mike. The Mike is aware this may happen. (Diagram 10-3)

DIAGRAM 10–3

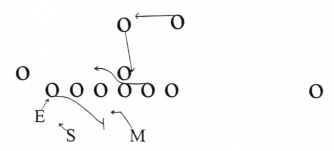

The right (weakside) defensive tackle attacks the center and attempts to keep him off the Mike. The defensive tackle reads the inside trap move by the left guard and slides toward the onside, remaining on the line of scrimmage. When he sees the halfback with the ball and knows it is not the Trap play, he can come across the line of scrimmage and attack the running back in the backfield. However, he must defeat the block of the fullback who is attempting to seal the weakside A gap. The only way the defensive tackle can beat the fullback's block is to slide along the line of scrimmage, with the left guard's pull, toward the strongside A gap. This movement by the defensive tackle makes the fullback's block very difficult. Often the weakside defensive tackle makes a tackle for a loss on the Sweep. (Diagram 10-4)

The right (weakside) defensive end realizes the ball is going away from him. The defensive end checks for the Waggle play and makes sure

DIAGRAM 10—4

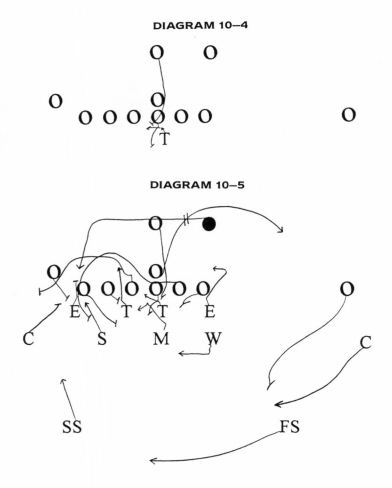

DIAGRAM 10—5

the quarterback has not kept the ball. Once the threat of the Waggle play
is gone, the defensive end trails the play looking for any reverse plays.

The Will reads the set halfback as his key. When the halfback flows
away and the Will sees the left guard cross the spot, he gets into his
hitman mode, moves to the onside, and gets into the proper pursuit
angle.

Once the threat of a pass is gone, the free safety rotates through
the deep middle zone and stays on the inside hip of the ballcarrier. He is
there to prevent any deep cutback by the ballcarrier.

The right corner, after the threat of pass has gone, takes the proper
angle to the ball. He, like the free safety, rotates through the secondary
and stays behind the ballcarrier. (Diagram 10-5)

DEFENDING THE SWEEP—
WITH THE
KEY BLITZ AND ORANGE COVERAGE

This is a good variation to use against the Wing-T Sweep. It allows
immediate penetration by the Mike and the strong possibility of a tackle
for a loss and very fast secondary run fill.

The four down defensive linemen react in the same manner as they
did in the Basic 4-3 front.

The three linebackers read the set halfback as their blitz key. When
the Sam reads the set halfback coming in his direction, he blitzes the
strongside C gap. This can present a problem for the Sam. Since the path
of the tight end has been altered by the strongside defensive end, the
tight end is releasing flatter to the line of scrimmage. This puts the tight
end in a better position to pick up the blitzing Sam. The Sam may be
blocked inside by the tight end and be ineffective versus the Sweep.
Hopefully, the Sam can beat the block of the tight end by quickness or
strength and get penetration into the backfield. Often, the Sam is taken
out of the play. (Diagram 10-6)

DIAGRAM 10—6

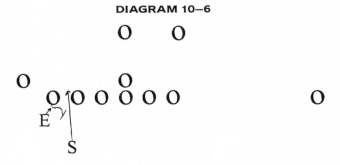

DIAGRAM 10—7

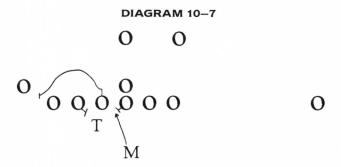

The Mike is most significant in this blitz. Once he reads his key, he blitzes into the strongside A gap. Since the center is being hit by the weakside defensive tackle, the center may be able to get a piece of the Mike but he cannot cut him off from penetrating. The center can merely force the Mike to go a bit wider to the onside. The Mike should be able to get penetration between the block of the center and the strongside defensive tackle. (Diagram 10-7) At best, the Mike can tackle the ballcarrier for a loss. At worst, the Mike can knock the pulling right guard off his track and eliminate him as a possible blocker on the perimeter.

The Will plays the same way he plays in the Basic front.

The left corner is covering the wing with man-to-man coverage at a depth of five yards. Once the corner recognizes the down block by the wing, he reacts up much faster than he did in the zone coverage (Cover 2–Blue Spot). The corner replaces the wing in the same manner as in Cover 2, and he is in an excellent position to make the play.

The strong safety is covering the tight end with man-to-man coverage, either from the Blue Spot alignment or from a depth of five yards. Once he recognizes the down block by the tight end, he reacts up to stop the play. The strong safety becomes an additional player on the line of scrimmage. This was not the case when the zone coverage (Cover 2–Blue Spot) was used.

The free safety moves to a true free-safety position, either in his initial alignment or after the snap of the ball when the Blue Spot alignment is employed. The free safety is a pass defender first and cannot attack the run until the threat of pass has disappeared. He must be very careful because he is the last line of defense to stop the ballcarrier and a possible TD.

The right corner, playing man to man on the split end (#1), stays with his man until the threat of a pass has gone. The offside corner is little help against the Sweep play. (Diagram 10-8)

DIAGRAM 10—8

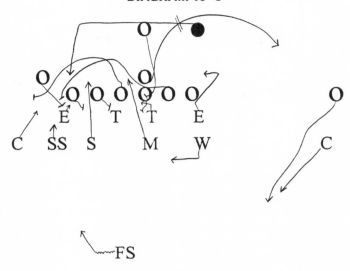

DEFENDING THE TRAP—
WITH THE
BASIC 4-3 WITH COVER 2

The left (strongside) defensive tackle is the key to stopping the Trap play. The Trap play can be executed with the right guard employing two different blocks. The guard may execute a false pull to the outside to simulate the Sweep or he might go inside in an attempt to block the Mike.

In this discussion of the Trap play, the inside move by the right guard is used. When the right guard steps inside to block the Mike, it is a simple read for the left defensive tackle. The movement of the guard forces the defensive tackle to turn slightly to the inside in order to get a good piece of the guard in an attempt to keep him off the Mike. This slight turn puts the defensive tackle in the perfect position to wrong arm the trapping left guard and force the fullback to bounce to the outside. (Diagram 10-9) The defensive tackle is expected to pursue the fullback when the fullback is forced to bounce the play to the outside by the wrong-arm technique.

The left (strongside) defensive end reads the base block of the tight end and forces him into the C gap. When the defensive end realizes it is the Trap play, he pursues the play. Often, the defensive end is involved in making the tackle when the fullback is forced to bounce to the outside.

DIAGRAM 10—9

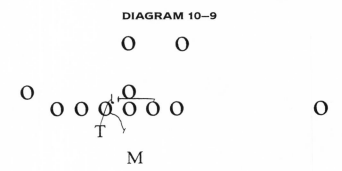

The Sam reads the far-set halfback. When he sees his key coming toward him and the left guard cross the spot, he assumes the play is Sweep. However, when the right offensive tackle attempts to base block the Sam, the Sam realizes it is the Trap and not the Sweep. The Sam maintains control of the C gap and does not allow himself to be pushed back or outside by the block of the offensive tackle. When the fullback is forced to bounce to the outside, the Sam could be the first defender to make the tackle.

As the wing fakes the down block to simulate the Sweep, the left corner makes sure the wing is not attempting to fake a block and then release into the flat area for a pass. The corner must honor the possibility of pass before he commits to the run.

The strong safety is slow reacting to the running play. However, if the trap block is successful on the left defensive tackle and the Mike does not make the play, the strong safety is there to make the tackle. As in the Sweep, the ballcarrier will get at least a five-yard gain before the strong safety makes the play.

The Mike reads the initial move of the fullback to the defensive right. However, by reading the spot and seeing the left guard cross it, the Mike knows it is either the Sweep or the Trap. The Mike steps up (downhill) to defend the strongside A gap. If the strongside defensive tackle did a good job getting a piece of the right guard, the Mike can beat the down block of the guard and seal the A gap. If the right guard gets to the Mike, the Mike MUST push him to the onside or at least create a stalemate in the A gap. When the fullback bounces to the outside, the Mike may go across the face of the right offensive tackle to make the play.

The right (weakside) defensive tackle attacks the center, who is attempting to base block him. The defensive tackle pushes the center into the strongside A gap. By pushing the center into the strongside A gap, the defensive tackle constricts the strongside A gap. When the

DIAGRAM 10—10

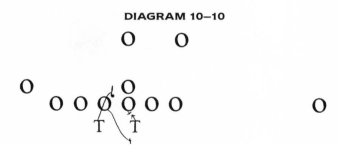

strongside defensive tackle executes a good wrong arm technique and the weakside defensive tackle forces the center into the strongside A gap, there is no room for the fullback to run inside. The fullback is forced to bounce to the outside. (Diagram 10-10)

The right (weakside) defensive end reacts in the same way he reacted to the Sweep.

The Will, initially, reacts in the same way he reacted to the Sweep. From his hitman technique, there is a good chance he can recognize the Trap and get in on the tackle. However, he cannot go to the onside too quickly and allow the possibility of a cutback run by the fullback.

The free safety and the right corner react in the same way they reacted to the Sweep. However, they do not flow to the onside quite as quickly since the Trap is not a perimeter play. (Diagram 10-11)

DIAGRAM 10—11

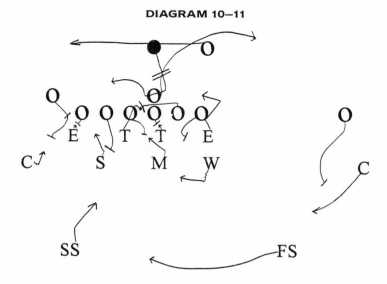

DEFENDING THE TRAP—
WITH THE
BASIC 4-3 WITH A WEAKSIDE ED IT
STUNT WITH COVER 2 (BLUE SPOT)

Except for the weakside defensive tackle and the weakside defensive end, the entire defense reacts to the Trap play in the way already described. However, the Ed It stunt, executed by the weakside defensive tackle and end, can cause a severe problem for the offensive team.

After slightly adjusting his alignment, the defensive end executes a gap charge through the weakside B gap. The left offensive tackle is in a poor position to prevent the penetration. The offensive tackle may get a piece of the defensive end and push the defensive end toward the onside and closer to the play. The center, who steps to block the defensive tackle, cannot make the block on the end. The center, normally, goes to the next level and attempts to block the Will. The end is free to collide with the fullback and make a big hit. This stunt allows the defensive end to make an outstanding play.

The weakside defensive tackle aligns in a 2i alignment and cheats to a nearly head-up position on the offensive left guard. The stunt takes the defensive tackle out of the play. However, he assumes the job of the defensive end and checks for the Waggle play. (Diagram 10-12)

DIAGRAM 10–12

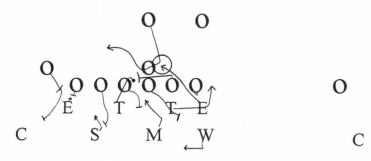

11

The 4-3 Vs. the Single-Back, Drop-Back Passing Game

The five- and seven-step drop-back passing game is part of most offensive arsenals. The two goals of every defensive team, in order to stop or seriously limit the passing game, are to execute excellent pass coverage while putting significant pressure on the quarterback. A key ingredient in achieving these lofty goals is to cause confusion for the offensive team, particularly the quarterback. In the 4-3 Defense, there are numerous ways to accomplish this feat. Some of these methods are analyzed in this section of the text.

In this chapter, the Single-Back, Drop-Back passing game is described from a Pro-Twins formation. The pro side of the offensive formation is to the defensive left and is considered the strongside of the formation. A five-step drop is used, with the following patterns employed by the offense:

- Flanker—Curl
- Tight End—Flat and Wheel
- Slot—Drag
- Split End—Deep Post (Diagram 11-1)

DIAGRAM 11–1

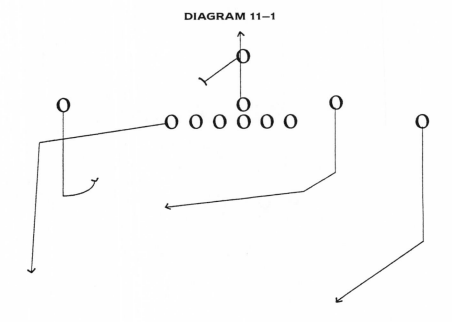

DEFENDING THE SINGLE-BACK,
DROP-BACK PASSING GAME—
WITH THE
BASIC 4-3 WITH COVER 2

The defensive line employs its basic alignments and executes its various pass-rush techniques.

The linebackers align in their Basic Alignments unless Trick is being employed.

Prior to the snap, the Sam recognizes the formation and sees the tight end (#2) and the flanker (#1) as possible threats to his area of pass coverage.

The tight end could run a vertical route and the Sam would have to hang inside the receiver until the tight end gets to a depth of twelve to sixteen yards. The Sam would then fly to the curl area. When the tight end executes a vertical release, there is a good chance the flanker is not running a curl pattern. This allows the Sam the time to stay with the tight end's possible vertical pattern until the tight end reaches a twelve-to sixteen-yard depth.

The flanker could run a Curl pattern and the Sam would have to get under it. Normally, when the flanker executes a Curl pattern, the tight end employs a horizontal release. This type of tight-end release is a cue for the Sam to fly to the Curl area.

When the Sam recognizes a pass play, he looks directly to the tight end. He sees the tight end's horizontal release. The Sam, with his head on a pivot, sees the flanker and sprints directly to the Curl area where he undercovers the Curl pattern by the flanker. The Sam makes sure he defends the pattern by keeping himself between the quarterback and the flanker.

The left corner makes contact with #1 and attempts to disrupt the route of #1. The corner does this as he is reading the route of #2. When the corner sees the horizontal release of #2, the corner begins to drop to a depth of twelve yards. From this depth, the corner can come up if the ball is thrown to #2 (Flat route). The corner is also in a good position to cover #2 if he turns his pattern up (Wheel route).

The left corner sees the vertical release of #2 and drops to his appropriate depth. When #2 turns the pattern up, the corner covers #2 with man-to-man coverage.

The strong safety reads the route of #2. When the safety sees the horizontal release of #2, the safety slides to cover a deep pattern by #1. Since #1 executes the Curl pattern, and does not come into the deep one-half zone, the safety hangs back, knowing the Curl pattern is covered by the Sam. The strong safety sees the corner in man-to-man coverage with #2 and the safety stays deep to help cover this pattern. In this case, the strong safety is a true zone player. (Diagram 11-2)

DIAGRAM 11–2

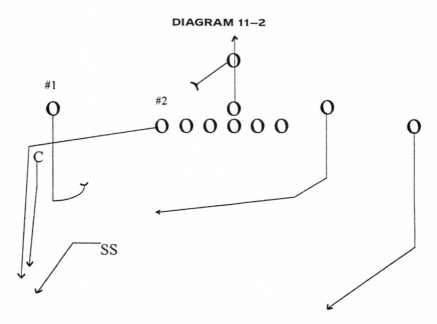

Prior to the snap, the Mike recognizes the possibility of vertical releases by both #2's and knows that if this occurs he must look at the head of the quarterback to determine his drop angle. The Mike recognizes a pass play and sees the tight end execute a horizontal release and the slot run a crossing pattern (Drag). Once the Mike sees the horizontal release of the tight end, he realizes his main threat to that side of the offensive formation is gone. The Mike sees the Drag pattern and gets underneath the pattern to prevent a short pass over the middle. Once the Drag pattern leaves his area of pass-coverage responsibility, the Mike looks for any other threat in his zone. He does not "cover grass" and looks for another receiver to cover.

The Will recognizes the formation and sees the slot (#2) and the split end (#1) as possible threats to his area of pass coverage. Since there is only one back in the backfield, the Will realizes there is a very slim possibility of two backs attacking the B gap. This allows the Will to widen his alignment and get a bit closer to the slot to discourage a quick pass to the slot.

The possible routes of #1 and #2 are the same possible routes as the tight end and flanker on the other side of the formation. When the

DIAGRAM 11–3

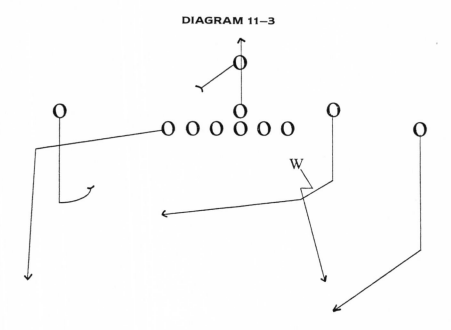

Will recognizes a pass play, he looks to the slot. When he sees the vertical release, the Will undercovers the Drag pattern until the slot leaves the Will's area of responsibility. The Will looks to #1 and sees a deep Post pattern. Since there is no other threat in the Will's zone, the Will continues to drop and ends up undercovering #1's Post pattern, while keeping a wary eye on his zone coverage area for any late crossing patterns. (Diagram 11-3)

The right corner makes contact with #1 (split end) and disrupts his pattern. He disrupts #1 as he is reading #2. As the corner sees #2 execute a vertical release, the corner covers #1 with man-to-man coverage. Knowing there is undercoverage by the Will, the corner is much more protective of a deep pattern than an underneath pattern.

The free safety reads #2 as his key. When #2 (slot) executes a vertical release, the free safety covers him with man-to-man coverage. Like the right corner, the strong safety knows there is underneath coverage. First, the Will undercovers the crossing route, and then the Mike undercovers the route. The free safety is primarily concerned about deep route and can afford to play a little looser than in a normal man-to-man situation. (Diagram 11-4)

DIAGRAM 11—4

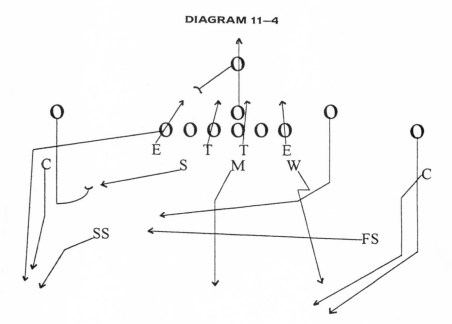

DEFENDING THE SINGLE-BACK,
DROP-BACK PASSING GAME—
WITH THE
FOUR BLITZ STRONG X WITH RED COVERAGE

The left (strongside) defensive tackle goes through the face of the right guard and rushes through the strongside A gap. The tackle may tighten his alignment slightly (almost nose to nose with the guard) to eliminate the possibility of being cut off by the guard.

A major part of the defensive tackle's job is to occupy the guard and prevent him from attempting to pick up the blitzing Mike. Depending on the pass-blocking scheme employed by the offense, the guard may attempt to leave the tackle for the center and look to pick up the Mike. (Diagram 11-5) Even if it slows down his pass rush, the defensive tackle cannot allow this to happen.

The left (strongside) defensive end executes his normal pass rush. He is very conscious of not constricting his pass-rush lane. This allows the blitzing Sam to have the C gap rushing lane to himself and keeps the defensive end as the outside contain defender. (Diagram 11-6)

DIAGRAM 11–5

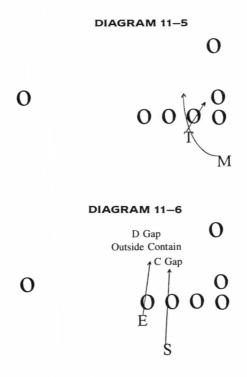

DIAGRAM 11–6

The Sam blitzes the strongside C gap. This may be executed from normal alignment or Show alignment. The Sam attempts to make contact with the right offensive tackle to stop or slow the tackle from picking up the Mike. After this job, the Sam tries to sack the quarterback or, at least, force the quarterback to hurry his pass.

The Sam may also be involved in pass coverage. The Sam blitzes toward the single setback. If the back goes out for a pass to the strongside, he becomes #3, and the Sam is responsible for covering him. This is part of the Sam's Blitz Peel responsibility. (Diagram 11-7) This is extremely important when the offense intends to execute a screen pass to the setback. The Sam makes contact with the setback, and then the setback attempts to slide out for a pass. The Sam must be able to feel for the screen pass and react accordingly.

The secondary executes man-to-man coverage (Red). This may be employed from the Blue Spot alignment or Red alignment. When it is employed from Blue Spot alignment, the safeties are aware of the possibility of a quick pass to either #2. When a quick pass is thrown, the safety comes up and makes a BIG HIT on the receiver and attempts to separate the receiver from the ball. When the Red alignment is used, the safeties are sure to inside cover the #2's and take away the quick pass.

The Mike aligns directly over the center, or moves to that alignment prior to the snap of the ball. The Mike cannot align too close to the strongside B gap before starting the blitz. When the Mike aligns too close to the B gap, the timing of the blitz can be thrown off, and the B gap may not open for the Mike. The Mike has no Blitz Peel responsibility and can blitz with reckless abandon.

On the snap of the ball, the Mike blitzes the strongside B gap and locates the ball. Since the left defensive tackle goes across the face of the right guard and controls the guard, the Mike blitzes as close to the

DIAGRAM 11-7

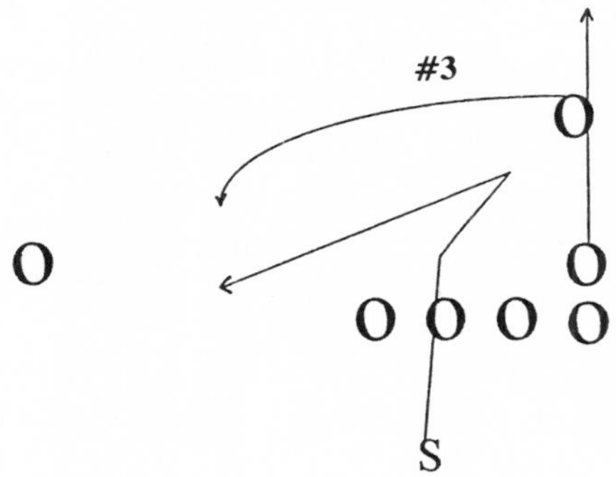

guard as possible to avoid a block of the right offensive tackle. Hopefully, the right offensive tackle will attempt to block the Sam, and this will leave the Mike free through the line of scrimmage. (Diagram 11-8) When the offensive tackle does block the Mike, the Sam should get through the line of scrimmage unblocked. (Diagram 11-9)

DIAGRAM 11—8

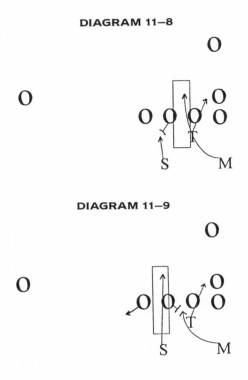

DIAGRAM 11—9

The right (weakside) defensive tackle and end execute their normal pass rush in the proper lanes. Since there are four defenders rushing from the strongside, the weakside defenders expect the quarterback to attempt an escape to the weakside and into their hands.

The Will executes his Basic techniques. However, since Red coverage is being employed, the Will is responsible for #3 to the weakside. When #3 does release to the weakside, the Will covers him with man-to-man coverage. The Will, since he is the only linebacker not blitzing, is mindful of the Draw Play and looks to the setback for this possibility.

When #3 does not release to his side, the Will plays a type of zone coverage. Unlike his normal area of zone responsibility, the Will drops

DIAGRAM 11–10

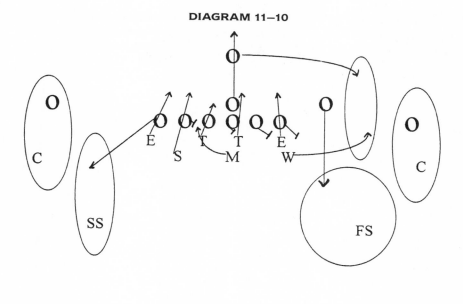

DIAGRAM 11–11

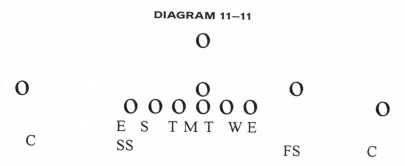

toward the middle of the formation and is looking for any crossing routes. (Diagram 11-10)

Since the offensive play described in this chapter is normally executed in a long-distance or passing situation, various disguises could be employed by the defensive team with the defenses described in this chapter. The secondary could execute the coverages from Blue Spot alignment or a variety of other alignments. The linebackers could use Show and/or Trick.

Employing Basic 4-3 with Cover 2 against this one-back formation, the defense could execute Blue Spot (Cover 2) from Red alignment, while the linebackers could employ Trick. (Diagram 11-11)

Employing Four Blitz Strong X with Red coverage against the one-back formation, the defense could execute the Red coverage with the corners in lock alignment, with the Sam in Show and the Will in Trick. (Diagram 11-12)

These are only two of the numerous disguise possibilities.

DIAGRAM 11—12

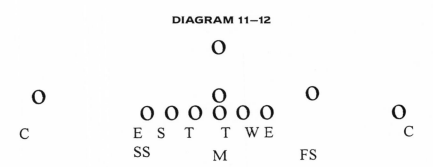

12

The 4-3 Vs. the I-Option Play

In football today, the Option is being executed from an infinite number of formations, and there are many different kinds of Option plays. In this chapter, the Triple Option is described from the Slot-I formation. It is described to the defensive left and to the weakside of the offensive formation. For the defensive front, the tight-end side is the strongside, and the slot side is the weakside. It is just the opposite for the secondary.

Many 4-3 defensive teams treat the tight slot like he was a weakside tight end. This puts the weakside defensive tackle in a 1 alignment, the end in a 5 alignment, and the Will in a 7 alignment. (Diagram 12-1)

DIAGRAM 12—1

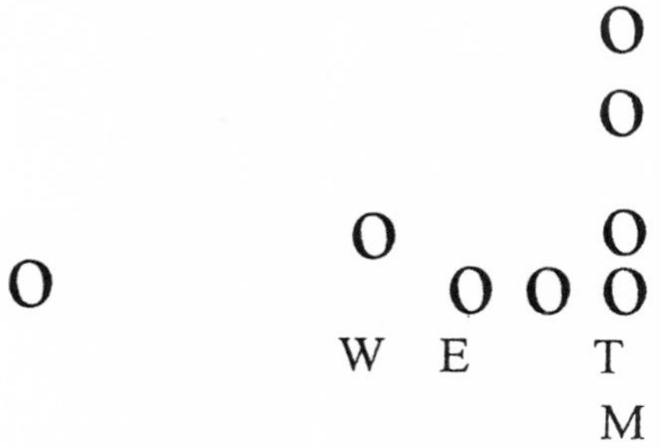

```
                          O
                          O

              O               O
O                 O O O
          W   E       T
                      M
```

DEFENDING THE TRIPLE OPTION—
WITH THE
BASIC 4-3 WITH COVER 2

The left (weakside) defensive tackle attacks the center and feels for a down block (double team) by the right guard. When the defensive tackle feels the double-team block, he attacks the guard. Since the defensive tackle has worked against the Option-blocking schemes all week, he knows the guard will attempt to chip block onto the Mike. The defensive tackle does everything he can to prevent the guard from chipping to the Mike. The defensive tackle does this while keeping his shoulders square to the line of scrimmage. He cannot allow himself to be moved off the line of scrimmage or toward the offside. If he is moved, either off the line of scrimmage or to the offside, a large crease develops in the B gap, and this gives the fullback, if given the ball, a large hole in which to run. The defensive tackle must force the guard into the B gap as much as possible.

The left (weakside) defensive end attacks the offensive tackle and prevents him from getting an easy release to the Mike. The defensive end steps inside with the tackle and attacks the first backfield threat. The defensive end is expected to tackle the first man with the ball. He normally tackles the fullback, and this eliminates a handoff to the fullback. However, when the quarterback makes an incorrect read and pulls the ball from the fullback prematurely, the defensive end can attack the quarterback. The end must stop the fullback FIRST! When the end plays a guessing game with the quarterback, the fullback may end up with a long gain. (Diagram 12-2)

The Will reads the arc release of the slot, as he reads the fullback (near back). The Will steps out and back with the slot. However, the Will only widens slightly so as not to create a crease in the C gap. As the Will

DIAGRAM 12–2

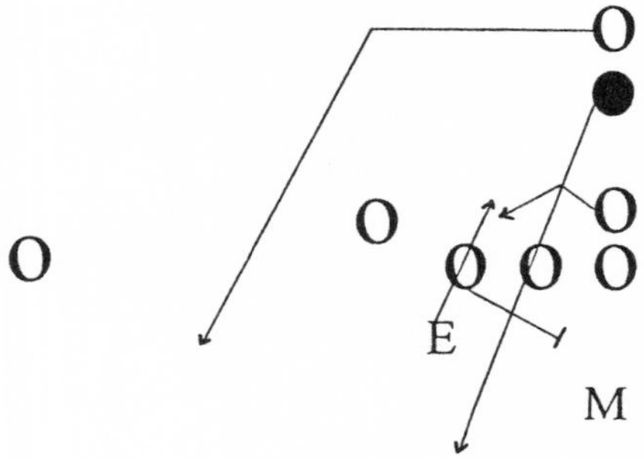

widens, he steps back off the line of scrimmage to a depth of two yards. The Will is coached to attack the next ball threat, and this is normally the quarterback. Since the Will is off the line of scrimmage, it is a difficult read for the quarterback. From the depth of two yards, the Will can attack the quarterback when he attempts to turn up in the C gap, and he can fly to the pitch when the quarterback pitches to the tailback. The off-the-line technique slows the quarterback's "pitch or keep" read and allows pursuit to catch up with the play. This technique is often referred to as a "Cat" technique. The Will never comes across the line of scrimmage to attack the quarterback. This type of attack would cause a fast pitch and does not allow the pursuit to develop.

The left corner reads the Option and is responsible for the back receiving the pitch. He attacks the play from the outside-in. Like the Will, he never crosses the line of scrimmage. When the corner stays two yards off the line of scrimmage, he creates a smaller lane for the tailback, if the tailback receives the pitch. This smaller lane also causes the tailback to turn up closer to the pursuit. If the corner crosses the line of scrimmage, the lane for the tailback is much wider and the tailback may outrun the pursuit to the perimeter. (Diagrams 12-3 and 12-4)

DIAGRAM 12—3

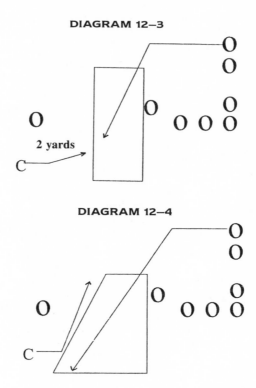

2 yards

DIAGRAM 12—4

The slot attempts to block the defender who is responsible for the pitch. Once the slot recognizes Cover 2, he adjusts his angle to kick the corner out. The corner meets the slot with his inside shoulder, while keeping his shoulders parallel to the line of scrimmage, and forces the tailback to run inside the block of the slot or into the pursuit. The corner cannot allow himself to be pushed outside or cannot allow himself to be knocked off his feet. Once the tailback turns upfield, the corner gets rid of the slot and attacks the ballcarrier.

The strong safety must be sure it is a run before committing to the line of scrimmage. When the pitch is made, the strong safety has to stay back for fear of a tailback pass to the split end (#1). (Diagram 12-5) Once the player with the ball (fullback, quarterback, or tailback) crosses the line of scrimmage, the strong safety fills from the inside-out.

In order to stop the Option, the defense must have the same or greater number of people at the perimeter as the offense. This is where the Mike comes into play. If the Option gets to the perimeter, the offense has the quarterback, tailback, and the slot there. So far, the defense has only the corner and the Will. The Mike has to be the third defender. Versus this formation and the Triple Option, the Mike slightly alters his alignment and moves more to the weakside to protect the B gap and to be a bit closer to the perimeter. Since the defensive end has closed the B gap and taken the fullback, when the tackle stepped inside to attack the Mike, the Mike has the freedom to continue to the outside. The Mike has to tackle the person with the ball. If the quarterback turns upfield, the Mike is there to help the Will with the tackle. If the quarterback pitches to the tailback, the Mike is there to attack the tailback from the inside-out. He is there to help the corner with the tackle.

In certain situations, versus the Triple Option, the Mike is assigned the quarterback and the Will is assigned the back receiving the pitch. This is a change from the basic way of playing the Option, but it is commonly employed. In this defensive scheme, the corner knows he has help with the pitch, prior to the snap of the ball, and the corner can play with reckless abandon. (Diagram 12-6)

The right (strongside) defensive tackle and end execute their normal reads and react accordingly. The defensive tackle must get into his pursuit angle as quickly as possible.

The Sam reacts to the movement of the fullback and begins his hitman technique. He is very conscious of a handoff to the fullback and a cutback to the offside (offensive left) A gap.

Once the threat of pass is gone, the free safety rotates through the deep middle zone and looks for the ballcarrier. The free safety cannot commit to the run too soon as he must wait for the possibility of a tailback pass.

The right corner, after the threat of pass has gone, takes the proper angle to the ball. (Diagram 12-7)

DIAGRAM 12–5

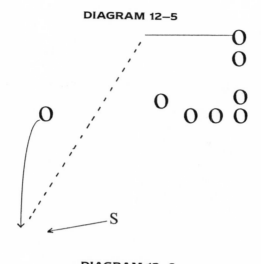

DIAGRAM 12–6

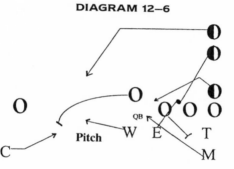

DIAGRAM 12–7

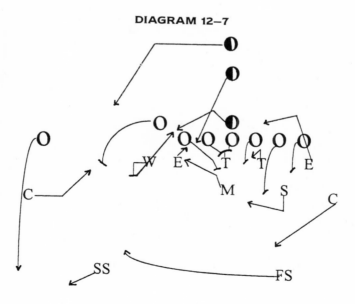

DEFENDING THE TRIPLE OPTION—
WITH THE
WEAK FRONT AND GREEN FLOW COVERAGE

The left (weakside) defensive tackle, in a 3 alignment, is closer to the point of attack for the fullback handoff and must be moved off the line of scrimmage or toward the offside for the fullback handoff to be effective. When aligned in a 1 technique (Basic), the defensive tackle did not present as big a problem to the offense as he does in a 3 alignment.

The defensive tackle attacks the right guard, expecting the double-team block from the right offensive tackle. The defensive tackle also knows, from working against the various Option blocking schemes during the practice week, that the offensive tackle will attempt to chip block to the Mike. The defensive tackle attacks the offensive tackle on the double-team block and tries to keep him from chipping to the Mike. The defensive tackle attempts to jam the offensive tackle into the B gap. When successful, the defensive tackle forces the fullback to run wider than he would like to run. Never giving ground is the goal of the defensive tackle.

The left (weakside) defensive end, in a 7 alignment, steps parallel to the line of scrimmage with his outside foot and keeps his inside foot in place against the slot arc block. Upon recognition of the Option, the defensive end steps back off the line of scrimmage, attempting to give the quarterback a difficult keep or pitch read. This off-the-line technique gives the other defenders time to pursue to the ball. Like the Will in Basic, the defensive end employs a Cat technique. When the quarterback turns up into the C gap with the ball, the end can make the play. When the quarterback pitches to the tailback, the end can sprint to the ballcarrier and help make the play.

The Will, in a 50 alignment, reads the movement of the fullback and the down block by the offensive tackle. The Will is responsible for the C gap and must step up to take the fullback. With the quarterback reading the Will, aligned off the line of scrimmage, as his keep or handoff key, the ball is often given to the fullback. [A way to eliminate this read is to align the Will in a Trick alignment. This makes the read of the quarterback a bit more difficult. (Diagram 12-8)] The Will has to step up and collide with the fullback, when he is sure the fullback has the ball. He cannot allow the fullback to gain yardage due to his slow reaction to the play. When the ball is not given to the fullback, the Will shifts his attention to the quarterback to look for the keep or pitch. The Will attacks the offensive player with the ball.

Green Flow coverage is used versus Option offenses. It is executed from the Blue Spot alignment. The secondary rotation is predicated on

DIAGRAM 12–8

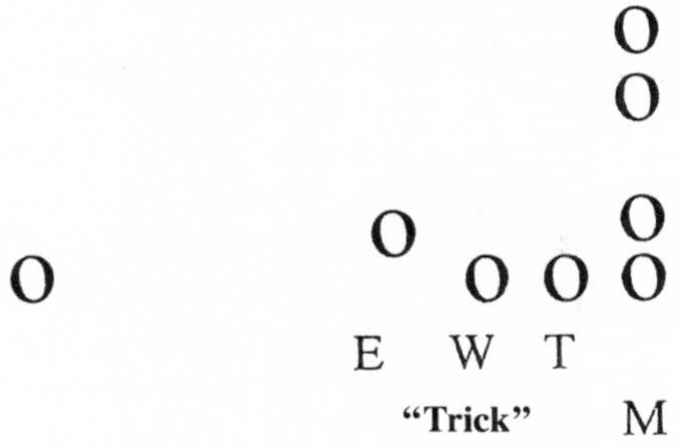

O

O

      O   O

O   O O O

          E   W   T

          "Trick"   M

the movement of the fullback. When the fullback moves toward the split end and the Option is being executed to the two-receiver side, Sky coverage is employed (safety responsible for pitch). When the fullback moves toward the tight end and the Option is being executed to the single tight-end side, Cloud coverage is employed (corner responsible for pitch).

For the left corner, Green Flow coverage is the same as Green Spot coverage. The corner is responsible for the deep outside one-third zone. On the snap of the ball, the corner begins to retreat to his zone coverage area. He cannot come up to attack the run until the ballcarrier crosses the line of scrimmage.

The strong safety reads the fullback as his key. When the key starts to the defensive left, the strong safety becomes the Curl-to-Flat player. From the Blue Spot Alignment, the safety rotates up. Upon recognition of the secondary rotation, the slot attempts to block the strong safety, recognizing the strong safety as the defender assigned to pitch. The strong safety has to beat the block of the slot and play two yards off the line of scrimmage and defend against the tailback if the tailback receives the pitch. The strong safety cannot allow himself to be pinned inside or kicked out. Normally, the slot attempts to pin the safety inside to create an outside running lane for the tailback to outrun the pursuit.

The free safety rotates to the deep middle one-third zone and plays as a true three-deep zone-free safety. Once he is free to attack the run, the free safety becomes an alley player and attacks the play from the inside-out. Often, the free safety becomes an extra defender on the perimeter and helps the defense outnumber the offense at the point of attack.

For the right corner, Green Flow coverage is the same as Green Spot coverage. He is responsible for the deep outside one-third zone. Upon recognition of run, he flows through the secondary and prevents any deep cutback run.

When the Option is run to the tight-end side of the formation, the secondary rotation is a bit different. Due to the alignment of #1, the corner is responsible for the pitch and the free safety takes the deep outside one-third zone. The strong safety moves to the deep middle one-third zone and becomes a true free safety. The left corner's area of responsibility remains the same. (Diagram 12-9)

Even with the Weak Front employed, the Mike still cheats his alignment sightly to the slot side of the formation in order to be in a better position to get to the perimeter. The Mike is responsible for the offensive right A gap. However, in the Weak Front, the Mike is able to flow more quickly to the outside, since he can read an A gap running play faster than the B gap running play he is responsible for in the Basic Front. The Mike is ready to defeat or avoid the block of the right offensive tackle. In the Basic Front, the right offensive tackle is hit by the left defensive end, and this delays the tackle's block on the Mike. In the Weak Front, the offensive tackle has a quicker release on the left defensive tackle and is quicker in his attempt to chip to the Mike. (Diagram 12-10) The Mike is expected to be another extra defender on the perimeter when the ball is not given to the fullback.

DIAGRAM 12–9

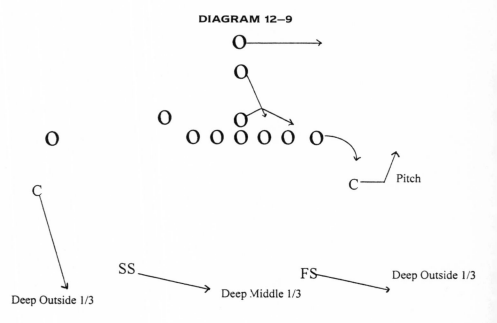

DIAGRAM 12–10

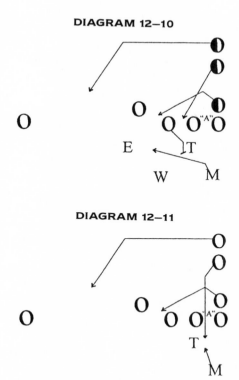

DIAGRAM 12–11

The Mike makes sure the fullback is not given the ball on an A gap dive. The Mike is responsible for this play before he considers going to the perimeter. (Diagram 12-11)

The right (strongside) defensive tackle attacks the base block of the center and jams him into the opposite A gap. When this is done correctly, the possibility of a successful A gap dive is eliminated. The defensive tackle begins to pursue as quickly as possible.

The right (strongside) defensive end plays the normal 5 alignment techniques and checks for any reverse plays. There are times when the onside defenders do a good enough job in forcing the quarterback to make slow reads so that the defensive end catches the quarterback from behind before he pitches the ball.

The Sam reacts to the running play and gets into his hitman mode. From his 7 alignment, he drops back and looks for any cutback or counter play and does not pursue to the onside too quickly. (Diagram 12-12)

DIAGRAM 12–12

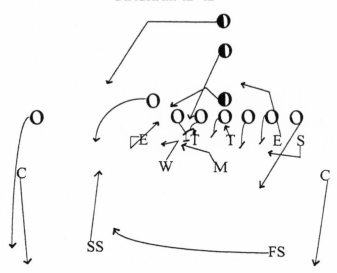

13

The 4-3 Vs. the Counter-Gap Play

The Counter-Gap Play has become one of the most-used plays in football today. It was made famous by the Washington Redskins of the National Football League and is used by professional, collegiate, and scholastic football teams throughout the United States. It is known by several different names. The Redskins Counter and the Counter Trey are two of the most common names. One interesting feature of this play is that it can be executed from numerous formations, and it can be run to both the strongside and weakside of a formation.

In this chapter, the Counter Gap is described to the weakside of the Pro-I formation and to the defensive right.

DEFENDING THE COUNTER GAP—
WITH THE
BASIC 4-3 WITH COVER 2

There are two crucial defensive elements involved in stopping the Counter Gap. The defensive end MUST WRONG ARM the lead block, and the linebackers, particularly the Mike and the Will, MUST READ THE SPOT. These two elements are discussed in detail in this chapter.

The right (weakside) defensive tackle attacks the center and feels for a down block by the left offensive guard. The center attempts to avoid the right defensive tackle and attacks the left defensive tackle. The right defensive tackle has to be more concerned about the left guard than the center. The defensive tackle forces the guard into the weakside B gap. The defensive tackle cannot allow himself to be driven to the offside. The tackle must, at least, create a stalemate with the offensive guard and not be moved. If the tackle is driven to the offside, a large crease develops between himself and the right defensive end, and a running lane opens for the lead blocker and the running back.

The right (weakside) defensive end is the key player in stopping the Counter Gap. The play of the defensive end is similar to the play of the onside defensive tackle versus the Guard Trap. The movement of the left offensive tackle forces the defensive end to turn slightly to the inside in order to get his hands on the tackle and prevent the tackle from getting an unimpeded block on the Mike. The slight turn of the defensive end puts him in a perfect position to wrong arm the kick-out block of the right guard. The defensive end, by wrong arming, forces the guard to execute a log block rather than a kick-out block. This is not a simple task for the guard. This forces the lead blocker (left offensive tackle) and the ballcarrier to go outside, rather than turn up inside where the play is designed to go. Once the defensive end forces the ballcarrier to the outside, he pursues the play.

The Will sees his key (fullback) step to the opposite side. The Will begins to adopt the hitman technique until he sees an offensive player cross the spot. This offensive movement tells the Will the play is coming to his side and he is now an onside linebacker, rather than an offside linebacker, with B or D gap responsibility. The Will knows that one of the backs went to the other side of the formation and two backs will not go into the B gap. He realizes he has D gap (outside) responsibility. However, the Will does not fly to the outside but freezes and reads the movement of the ballcarrier. When the right defensive end does his job, the ballcarrier and a blocker are forced to the outside. The Will is in position to attack the lead blocker (right offensive tackle) with the wrong-arm technique and force the ballcarrier to continue to the outside and to the waiting right corner. (Diagram 13-1) Once the Will forces the ballcarrier to the outside, he pursues the play.

The right corner reads the run and reacts to it. He attacks the

DIAGRAM 13—1

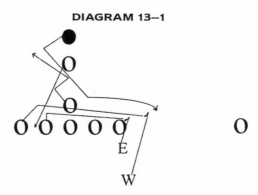

ballcarrier from the outside-in. The corner comes no closer than two yards from the line of scrimmage, but he moves to the inside, reducing the lane where the ballcarrier may run and forcing the ballcarrier into the defensive pursuit. When the right defensive end and the Will do their jobs correctly, the corner is left unblocked, with an opportunity to make an excellent defensive play. (Diagram 13-2)

DIAGRAM 13—2

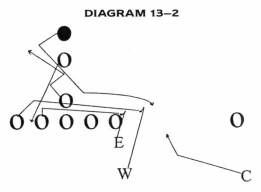

The free safety cannot commit to run too quickly as the ballcarrier could throw a pass to the split end (#1). Once he commits to the run, the free safety comes up, under control, to the outside. He comes up to the outside because the corner went to the inside. However, if the free safety is forced to make the play, the ballcarrier has made a significant gain.

The Mike sees his key move to the defensive left. Like the Will, the Mike sees an offensive player from the defensive left cross the spot. The Mike realizes the play is being executed to the defensive right, and he steps toward the onside B gap, and sees the oncoming left offensive tackle. The Mike beats the block of the tackle or, since he has no cutback responsibility, crosses the face of the blocker. The Mike can be, and often is, the player who stops this play. (Diagram 13-3)

DIAGRAM 13—3

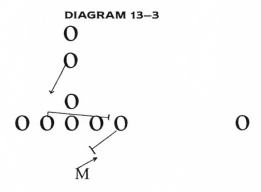

Reading of the spot by the Mike truly illustrates the value of this unique technique. Many teams, employing the 4-3 Defense, exclusively read the backs and blocking schemes. Reading the spot, after reading the near back as an initial key, is much simpler to execute and much simpler to teach. The Counter-Gap Play was one of the main reasons for the implementation of this type of read. A key ingredient for offensive success with the Counter Gap is to get the Mike moving the wrong way and too far out of position to react back to the play. Reading the spot gets the Mike flowing toward the play much quicker than reading and recognizing a blocking scheme, after the initial near-back read.

The left (strongside) defensive tackle attacks the right guard and reads his inside pull. The defensive tackle steps with his inside foot, parallel to the line of scrimmage. He collides with the center and attempts to force the center into the opposite A gap. The defensive tackle cannot cross the face of the center in an attempt to pursue the play. The tailback (ballcarrier) could cut the play back to the offside, and the defensive end has to be there to stop the play.

The left defensive end reacts to base block by the tight end. Since the play is away from him, the defensive end executes his normal offside techniques. He trails the play looking for a cutback.

The Sam, executing his hitman technique, must be mindful of a cutback by the tailback. Often, when the tailback (ballcarrier) sees the defensive end wrong arm the play, he attempts to cut the play back rather than run to the outside. The left defensive tackle and the Sam are there to stop the play. (Diagram 13-4) The Sam has to be mindful of the fullback, who seals the line of scrimmage for the pulling right offensive tackle. The fullback could come across the line of scrimmage, outside the left defensive tackle, and attempt to block the Sam.

DIAGRAM 13—4

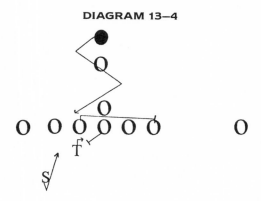

DIAGRAM 13—5

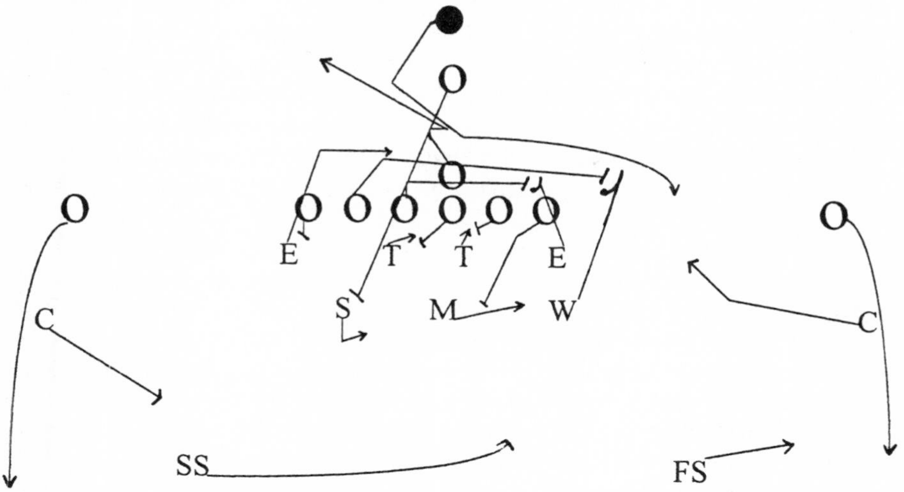

The strong safety flows through the deep middle zone and looks for deep cutback.

The left corner, like the strong safety, rotates through the secondary and stays behind the play. (Diagram 13-5)

DEFENDING THE COUNTER GAP—
WITH THE
THREE BLITZ WEAK X AND RED COVERAGE

The right (weakside) defensive tackle, because of the blitz, employs a tight (almost nose on nose with the offensive guard) 2i alignment. On the snap of the ball, the defensive tackle goes across the face of the left guard. The angle and ferocity of the defensive tackle's charge prohibits the guard from keeping the tackle out of the B gap. The defensive tackle must be careful not to get penetration before he knows whether the offensive play is a pass or run. As the left offensive tackle, on his path to the Mike, passes the defensive tackle, the defensive tackle gets an indication the play is a run. If the play was a passing play, the offensive tackle would not be leaving the line of scrimmage. (Diagram 13-6) The defensive tackle avoids penetration and, immediately, looks and turns slightly to the inside. From this position, the tackle wrong arms the kick-out blocker (right guard) and forces the ballcarrier to bounce to the outside.

The right (weakside) defensive end attacks the left offensive tackle and slows the tackle from a quick release onto the Mike. Since the offensive tackle releases off the line of scrimmage, the defensive end knows the play is not a passing play. Knowing the blitz and the movement of the defensive tackle, the defensive end does not expect to encounter a kick-out block. He knows, if a kick-out block is attempted, it should be directed at the defensive tackle who is in the B gap. The defensive end does not get penetration as he waits to see what running play develops.

When the defensive tackle does his job correctly, the tailback either bounces to the outside, where he is met by the defensive end, or cuts the play back to the inside. When the play is bounced to the outside, the defensive end attacks the lead blocker (right offensive tackle) with the wrong-arm technique and forces the ballcarrier to continue outside. The defensive end then pursues the ballcarrier.

On the snap of the ball, the Will blitzes the weakside A gap. Several offensive scenarios could occur involving the Will. When the left offensive guard makes a good attempt at blocking the right offensive tackle, the guard forfeits the possibility of picking up the blitzing Will. This allows the Will to get into the backfield and either make the tackle or knock off one of the pulling blockers. (Diagram 13-7)

The left offensive tackle, on his way to the Mike, could meet the Will and push him toward the gap the Will intends to blitz. This slightly disrupts the angle of the Will's blitz, but it allows the Mike an unimpeded path to the play, and the Will could still make the play or disrupt one of the pulling blockers. (Diagram 13-8)

The right corner, in the Blue Spot alignment, covers the split end (#1) with man-to-man coverage. He stays with the split end until the ballcarrier crosses the line of scrimmage.

The free safety, from the Blue Spot alignment, covers #2 to the weakside; #2 turns out to be the tailback. The free safety comes up on the play and acts like a linebacker. He becomes the unblocked defender at the point of attack. Since the original alignment of the free safety is between #1 and #2, the free safety attacks the play from the outside-in. When the defensive tackle and defensive end do their wrong-arm techniques correctly, the free safety makes the tackle on the perimeter. (Diagram 13-9)

The Mike's attack is very similar to his attack in the Basic Front. Unlike the Basic Front, the center is uncovered and goes directly to the Mike. The Mike, reading and reacting to the spot, should be able to beat this block and get to the onside.

If the left offensive tackle has made contact with the Will and is blocking him toward the weakside A gap, the Mike avoids them and is

DIAGRAM 13—6

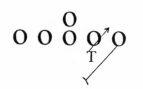

DIAGRAM 13—7

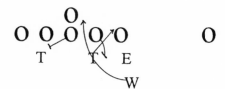

DIAGRAM 13—8

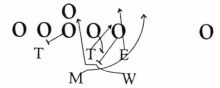

DIAGRAM 13—9

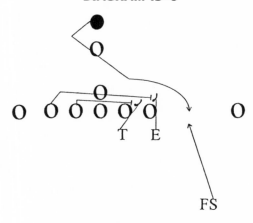

DIAGRAM 13—10

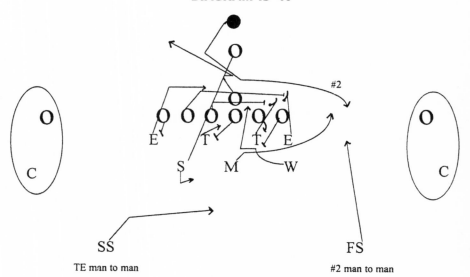

TE man to man   #2 man to man

free to the play. When the defensive tackle and end do their jobs correctly, the Mike attacks the ballcarrier on the perimeter from the inside-out and gets to that point unblocked. There is a strong possibility the Mike and the free safety will arrive on the perimeter and be two on one with the ballcarrier.

The left (strongside) defensive tackle and the left (strongside) defensive end play the same way in this defense as they do in the Basic Front.

The Sam, in Red coverage, is responsible for #3 to his side; #3 is the fullback. The Sam looks to cover the fullback on a pass route before making sure the play is a running play and assuming the hitman technique. Once the Sam recognizes the play as a running play, he plays in the same way he plays in the Basic Front.

The strong safety, from Blue Spot alignment, covers the tight end (#2) with man-to-man coverage. When he sees the tight end block the defensive end, and is sure the tight end is not executing a delay route, the strong safety comes up to cover the run. The strong safety starts up to the offside. When he recognizes the run is to the weakside, he adjusts his angle and attacks the play from the inside-out.

The left corner, in Blue Spot alignment, covers the split end (#1) with man-to-man coverage. He stays with the split end until the ballcarrier crosses the line of scrimmage. (Diagram 13-10)

14

The 4-3 Vs. the No-Back, Three-Step Passing Game

The best defense to employ versus the No-Back set is some form of Nickel Defense. However, when an offense employs a No-Back set as a change-up, rather than as a basic set, the defense must use the defensive personnel in the game.

The Basic 4-3 with Cover 2 is certainly not the best defense to use versus the No-Back set. The offensive set presents too many receivers on or near the line of scrimmage to be effectively defended with Cover 2. The Sam is put in a bind because #2 and #3 are on or near the line of scrimmage and both are threats to catch a quick pass. (Diagram 14-1) Many 4-3 defensive teams do not employ Cover 2 versus a Trips formation, but check to Green. This allows the Sam to move out on #3, and the strong safety to be aligned in a good position to discourage a quick pass to #2. (Diagram 14-2)

DIAGRAM 14—1

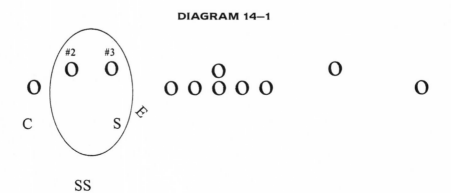

DIAGRAM 14-2

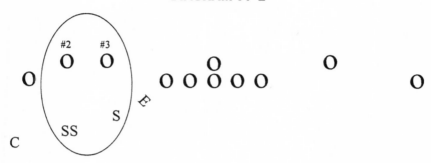

In this chapter, the Three-Step Passing game is described from a double-split-end offense with double slots to the defensive left (Trips and strongside) and a single slot to the defensive right (weakside). The quarterback employs a three-step drop with the following patterns employed by the offense:

- Strongside Split End (#1)—Out
- Outside Slot (#2)—Flag
- Inside Slot (#3)—Vertical
- Weakside Slot (#2)—Drag
- Weakside Split End (#1)—Deep Post

The Basic 4-3 is used. However, the secondary is checked from Cover 2 to Green.

DEFENDING THE NO-BACK, THREE-STEP PASSING GAME— WITH THE BASIC 4-3 WITH GREEN COVERAGE

The defensive linemen employ their basic alignments and execute their various pass-rush techniques.

Once the formation is recognized, the linebackers and members of the secondary realize the chances for a passing play, as opposed to a running play, are great. As they adjust their alignments, they check to see the possible threats to their zones.

Since #3 is a split slot, the Sam moves out on the slot and plays on the slot's inside shoulder, at a depth of five yards. This alignment should discourage any quick pass to the inside slot (#3). This alignment also helps discourage a quick pass to the other inside slot (#2). (Diagram 14-3)

DIAGRAM 14–3

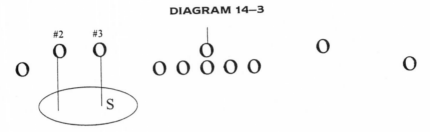

Once a passing play is recognized, the Sam reads the pattern of #3. When #3 executes a vertical route, Sam hangs inside of him to discourage a quick pass to #3. Since there are three receivers to the strongside, rather than two (a pro set), the Sam cannot hang with #3 beyond eight to ten yards. The Sam has to get to the Curl area, as the split end could be running a Curl pattern with the outside slot (#2) executing a horizontal release. (Diagram 14-4)

After the Sam leaves #3, he sees the vertical release by #2 and the out pattern by #1. The Sam drops between the vertical routes of #2 and #3. Since there is no Curl threat, the Sam hangs between the two receivers and continues to drop, keeping his eyes on the quarterback.

The left corner knows that in Green he is responsible for the deep outside one-third zone. When the corner reads the patterns of the Trips receivers, he sees the vertical routes by #2 and #3. The corner favors the route of #2, and the corner breaks on the Flag pattern. The corner is sure to stay deeper than the receiver. This prohibits the quarterback from throwing a deep ball and allowing the receiver to run under it.

The strong safety, who is responsible for the Curl area in Green coverage, sees the vertical releases of #2 and #3. The strong safety hangs on the outside shoulder of #2, keeping himself in a position to break on any quick pass to any of the three receivers. Upon recognition of the Out pattern by the split end (#1), the strong safety breaks to get under the pattern. If the strong safety cannot get under the Out pattern, he, at least,

DIAGRAM 14–4

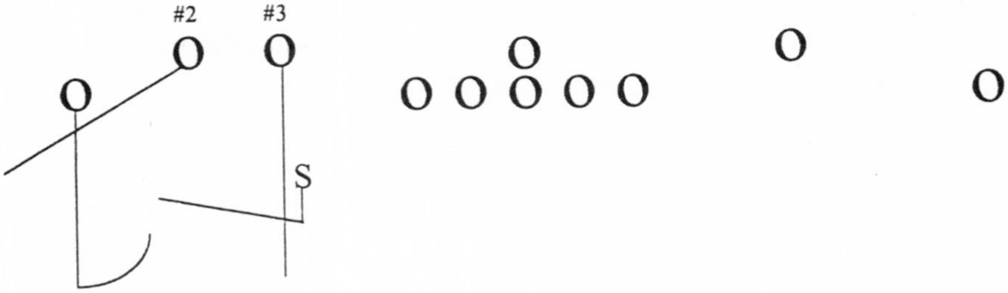

gets between the quarterback and the split end and forces the quarter-back to throw the Out pattern over him. This forces the quarterback to lob the pass over the strong safety, rather than fire it on a straight line. This forces a pass that is more susceptible to an interception.

On the snap of the ball, the free safety moves to an alignment two yards outside the original alignment of the strongside offensive tackle. From this position, the free safety sees the vertical releases of #2 and #3. Since the free safety is responsible for the deep strongside middle one-third zone, he pays particular attention to the pattern of #3 and moves toward that receiver. The free safety is not concerned with the weakside receivers, knowing the Will and the right corner are employ-ing man-to-man coverage on these receivers. Like the left corner, the free safety stays deeper than the receiver and keeps his eyes on the quarterback, while knowing the whereabouts of strongside #3.

The Mike, although in a zone coverage, is mainly concerned about the quarterback; he is responsible for the quarterback Draw play. As the Mike drops into coverage, he is aware of the vertical releases of strongside #3 and weakside #2. The Mike watches the quarterback's head to determine the angle of his drop. Mike ends up undercovering the Drag pattern by weakside #2, knowing the Will is employing man-to-man coverage on the receiver. Versus a No-Back set, the Mike has to be concerned about the quarterback FIRST and then the receivers.

The Will employs man-to-man coverage on the weakside slot #2 and is sure to take away the quick inside route first.

The right corner employs man-to-man coverage on the weakside split end. (Diagram 14-5)

DIAGRAM 14—5

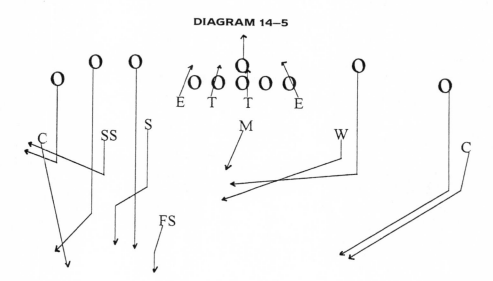

DEFENDING THE NO-BACK,
THREE-STEP PASSING GAME—
WITH
LOOSE STRONG, MIKE TRICK, AND
THREE BLITZ WEAK WITH RED COVERAGE

One method of retarding the progress of the 3-Step Passing game is to sack the quarterback. Since the quarterback is using only three steps, the pass defenders have to closely cover the receivers to prohibit quick completions, and the front defenders must get to the quarterback quickly. The 4-3 Defense provides numerous methods of accomplishing this goal.

The Loose stunt and the Three Blitz are two stunts that are effective versus this type of passing attack. The Red coverage allows the defenders to quickly cover the receivers while the front defenders are attacking the quarterback.

The left (strongside) defensive tackle executes his Basic alignment and his normal pass-rush techniques.

The left (strongside) defensive end aligns in a 7 alignment. In his alignment, the end aims at a point directly behind the right offensive tackle. On the snap of the ball, the end explodes toward that point and fights to get to the quarterback. Hopefully, the defensive end is a better and quicker athlete than the offensive tackle and can beat the offensive tackle with a good pass rush.

The Sam and the secondary are executing man-to-man coverage on their receivers. The defenders establish inside leverage on the receivers and prevent any quick-pass receptions. The quarterback is under pressure and has to pass quickly, and the defenders have to play great man-to-man coverage for a short period of time.

With this type of offense, the pass defenders may have to change receivers to get a better match-up. This is determined by the scouting report. The corner could play the #2 receiver, rather than the #1, if the #2 is the faster receiver. This prohibits executing the Red coverage from another alignment, but the advantages greatly outweigh the disadvantages.

The Mike aligns in a Trick alignment in the strongside A gap. This should force the center to attempt to block the Mike and not step to the weakside to pick up the right defensive tackle and spoil the weak blitz. On the snap of the ball, the Mike gets his hands on the center to draw his block. After getting hands on the center, the Mike is responsible for the quarterback. By touching the center, the Mike forces the center to attempt a block. Once the center realizes the Mike is not executing a blitz, although he may try, it is too late for the center to help the two

DIAGRAM 14—6

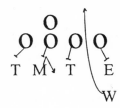

weakside blockers (left offensive guard and tackle) pick up the three defenders (right defensive tackle, end, and the Will). One of the three defenders (preferably the Will) should get in, untouched, and either sack the quarterback or force a bad throw. (Diagram 14-6)

Since the Mike is responsible for the quarterback, he could end up as an extra blitzer. Once the Mike reads the pass drop of the quarterback and he is sure the threat of the quarterback Draw play has passed, the Mike executes a delayed blitz. Since the Mike did not initially blitz from his Trick alignment, but merely touched the center, by the time the Mike does blitz, the center should have attempted to block elsewhere. This leaves a huge hole in the strongside A gap for the Mike to blitz. (Diagram 14-7)

The right (weakside) defensive tackle, in a 2i alignment, rushes through the inside shoulder of the left offensive guard. The tackle makes sure the offensive guard stays with him and does not step to the B gap. The purpose of the blitz is to get the Will in the backfield as quickly as possible. The defensive tackle may have to give up his pass rush to prevent the guard from blocking the Will.

The right (weakside) defensive end executes his normal pass rush. Like the right defensive tackle, the end forces the offensive tackle to block him and not step to the B gap. The end may also have to give up his pass rush in order to keep the B gap open for the blitzing Will.

DIAGRAM 14—7

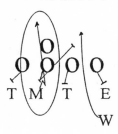

The Three Blitz is employed to get the Will to the quarterback. The Will from his wide alignment (No-Back set allows the Will to move out toward the weakside slot), sneaks his way to the B gap, prior to the snap of the ball. The Will blitzes the B gap and gets to the quarterback. (Diagram 14-8)

The defensive alignment, prior to the snap of the ball, gives the impression the weakside B gap is not defended. If the quarterback intends to execute a Draw play, the weakside B gap appears to be the best location for the play. The Three Blitz puts the Will in a great position to really smack the quarterback on a Draw play. (Diagram 14-9)

DIAGRAM 14—8

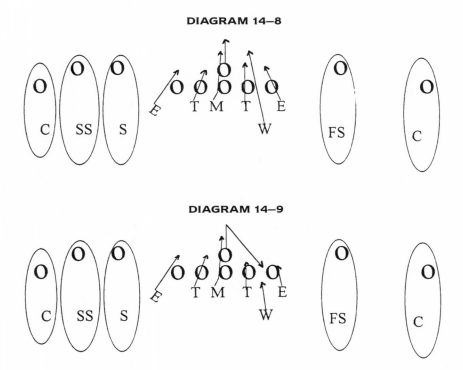

DIAGRAM 14—9

COACHING THE DEFENSIVE LINE
Fritz Shurmur

Fritz Shurmur, defensive coordinator for the Green Bay Packers, has written the definitive book for coaching a successful defensive line regardless of the level of play.

"I'm glad Fritz Shurmur is on my side. He's an excellent teacher, who also knows how to motivate. His books on defensive football must be part of every coach's library. Fritz is one of the best coaches I've ever worked with. Coaching the Defensive Line *is a must read."*

> Mike Holmgren
> Head Football Coach
> Green Bay Packers

*"*Coaching the Defensive Line *is another must read for all coaches and fans of fundamental football. It's a terrific tool for coaches at any level. From basic fronts, proper stance and drills, to the mental preparation needed, Fritz Shurmur covers all there is to know. This book is the 'Bible' of defensive line play."*

> Matt Millen
> TV Football Analyst
> Fox Sports

"Fritz Shurmur is more than a great football coach. He is a great teacher. I have read his other outstanding books and now he has written another. If you want to learn from the best, you will want to read Coaching the Defensive Line! *It is outstanding!"*

> Lloyd Carr
> Head Football Coach
> U. of Michigan

Fritz Shurmur has been a defensive coordinator for 17 of his 22 seasons in the NFL. In addition to his distinguished coaching career. Coach Shurmur is widely respected as the author of *Coaching Team Defense, Second Edition*, and *The Eagle Five-Linebacker Defense.*

$16.00

COACHING TEAM DEFENSE
Second Edition
Fritz Shurmur

Fritz Shurmur, the defensive coordinator for the Green Bay Packers, has expanded the original edition of his book, which is considered by many to be one of the best books ever written on football defense. This excellent guide provides a solid fundamental approach to understanding and executing the basic concepts of team defense.

"Coaching Team Defense, Second Edition, was and is a must for all coaches, players, and even fans who want to understand real football."

Matt Millen
TV Football Analyst
Fox Sports

"Fritz Shurmur's Coaching Team Defense—Second Edition expands on the first edition with diagrams, tackling and tackling drills, zone pass coverages, and everything not covered in the initial book. An excellent book for coaches at any level with explanations of all defensive areas."

George Perles
Former Head Coach
Michigan State U.

"Fritz Shurmur's new edition of Coaching Team Defense is an expanded version of truly one of the best books I've read regarding defensive football. The new book is full of clean and concise details of coaching defense that coaches of all levels will benefit from. This is Fritz's best work yet!"

Tom Hayes
Assistant Coach
Washington Redskins

Fritz Shurmur is a coaching veteran of more than 40 seasons, including 22 in the NFL. Coach Shurmur is also the author of *The Eagle Five-Linebacker Defense*.

$12.00

COACHING THE DEFENSIVE BACKFIELD
Greg McMackin

Coaching the Defensive Backfield is a thorough study of all the fundamentals, techniques and drills you will need to produce a successful secondary. You are shown the specific techniques and drills you will need to produce game-winning execution.

Coaching the Defensive Backfield allows you to prepare your secondary defenders through a complete plan concerning skills, techniques and game-like drills that will help you to produce a fundamentally sound, aggressive and exciting defensive backfield.

> *"Greg McMackin is one of the best in the business. His book is very informative and every coach should have one."*
>
> Dennis Erickson
> Head Coach—Seattle Seahawks

> *"This is the most comprehensive book I've read on secondary play...*Coaching the Defensive Backfield *will educate the coach and stimulate the player."*
>
> Ron McBride
> Head Coach—U. of Utah

> *"Pursuit, tackling, two deep, three deep, zone, man, blitz, bump...this book has it all.* Coaching the Defensive Backfield *is a must for coaches at all levels."*
>
> Steve Axman
> Head Coach
> Northern Arizona U.

Greg McMackin is the defensive coordinator for the Seattle Seahawks. Immediately prior to this, he served in the same capacity at the University of Miami where his defenses led the nation in several categories. Coach McMackin has coached successfully for more than 20 years at the high school, college and professional levels.

$12.00

THE EAGLE FIVE-LINEBACKER DEFENSE
Fritz Shurmur

Fritz Shurmur, defensive coordinator of the Green Bay Packers, presents a unique and innovative defensive scheme which is based on solid principles, techniques and drills that are applicable to any defensive plan at any level of play. This unique defensive concept allows coaches to attack today's wide-open offenses rather than having to react.

"If you want an exceptional version of modern-day defensive play, The Eagle Five-Linebacker Defense *by Fritz Shurmur is must reading."*

Bill Parcells
Head Football Coach
New England Patriots
Winner of Two Super Bowls

*"*The Eagle Five-Linebacker Defense *is a clear, concise, step-by-step discussion of an important trend in defensive football. If you want to be in the mainstream of defensive thinking, this book is must reading."*

Lloyd Carr
Head Football Coach
U. of Michigan

"Fritz Shurmur's The Eagle Five-Linebacker Defense *is a tremendous addition to any coach's library at any level of play. It is an excellent book on a unique way of utilizing defensive personnel in modern-day football."*

Tom Hayes
Assistant Coach
Washington Redskins

Fritz Shurmur is a coaching veteran of 40 years, including the last 20 in the NFL. Recognized as a defensive innovator, Coach Shurmur served as defensive coordinator with the Phoenix Cardinals and the Los Angeles Rams before coming to Green Bay. He is also the author of *Coaching Team Defense, Second Edition*.

$12.00

DEFENSING THE DELAWARE WING-T, Bob Kenig ($12.00)

This coaching guide offers a successful and easily teachable answer to the dynamic Wing-T. The innovative use of the 3-4 "Slant" and "Read Blitz" presents major problems for this offense. All aspects of installing the "Slant" and "Read Blitz" are detailed, and the actual application of these techniques is explained and diagramed against the basic Wing-T plays. Bob Kenig has coached successfully at both the high school and college levels. He is presently coaching at Widener University where he has helped them reach the NCAA Division III playoffs each of the past two seasons.

FOOTBALL'S EXPLOSIVE MULTI-BONE ATTACK, Tony DeMeo($12.00)

Coach DeMeo, who is presently the head coach at Washburn University, is widely recognized as one of the most innovative offensive coaches in football today. His Multi-Bone combines the explosiveness of the Veer, the power of the I, the deception and misdirection of the Wing-T, the ball control of the Wishbone and the wide-open play of the Pro Drop-back Passing game. This book shows you how to tie together the best of these offenses into one easy-to-learn package.

COACHING RUN-AND-SHOOT FOOTBALL, Al Black ($12.00)

This unique guide presents an exciting attack that can enhance your present offense or stand alone. Coach Black, a successful 30-year coaching veteran whose career includes a very impressive 149-41-2 high school record, gives you all the run-and-shoot pass routes, plus blocking schemes, a complementary offense, a one-back running game, and much more.

DEFENSING THE RUN AND SHOOT, Bob Kenig ($12.00)

Bob Kenig, author of the very popular **DEFENSING THE DELAWARE WING-T**, gives you the tools to derail the explosive Run and Shoot. The defensive system in this book employs both odd and even fronts, which are skillfully utilized with man-to-man, zone and combination defenses. The book also provides you with an extensive blitz package, plus an invaluable chapter that shows you how to disguise the defenses. Coach Kenig recently completed his latest book, *Football's Modern 4-3 Defense*, available from Harding Press January, 1997 ($18.00).

HARDING PRESS, INC.
P.O. BOX 141
HAWORTH, N.J. 07641
(201) 767-7114
FAX: (201) 767-8745

ORDER FORM

# of COPIES	TITLE	TOTAL PRICE

Postage & Handling: SUBTOTAL_____

Order	U.S.	Outside U.S.	
Under $25.00	$3.00	$ 7.75	NJ Residents –
$ 25.00 – $ 49.99	$4.75	$10.50	Add 6% Sales Tax _____
$ 50.00 – $ 74.99	$6.25	$11.75	
$ 75.00 – $ 99.99	$7.50	$12.75	P & H _____
$100.00 – $149.99	$8.25	$13.50	
$150.00 – $199.99	$9.00	$14.50	TOTAL _____
$200.00 +	$9.75	$15.00	

EACH ORDER MUST BE ACCOMPANIED BY CHECK, M.O., P.O., or CREDIT CARD info

COACH'S NAME _____

ADDRESS _____

_____

CITY _____ **STATE** _____ **ZIP** _____

PHONE # (____)_____
               area code

MASTERCARD/VISA: _____
                    Card #   **Exp. Date**

                    _____
                    Signature